Yet Another
101 Tales of a Middle-Class
Middle-Child

By Pete Zakroff

Edited by Terry Zakroff and Herb Levin

Artwork by Laura Tempest Zakroff

Yet another 101 Tales of a Middle-Class Middle-Child

Yet another 101 Tales of a Middle-Class Middle-Child

Special thanks to my wife, Terry, and our children, Stephen, Dennis, and Laura for their comments, suggestions, and support. I'd also like to thank Marcy Altimano, Sally Jack, Herb Levin, and Nate Rosenblatt for their efforts in helping to bring these latest stories to life. I would also be remiss if I didn't thank all the many characters I've met throughout my soap opera of an existence who knowingly or unknowingly provided me with much of the content for the tales in this tome.

Introduction

My Long Running Soap Opera

I'm not a fan of soap operas. In fact, I'm more a fan of horse and space operas. But looking back at my time and existence spanning the 20th and 21st centuries, my life has been one long soap opera that luckily keeps getting renewed. For how long? None of us really knows.

Here's what I mean. Take for instance the long running shows on TV such as Days of Our Lives, Law and Order, CSI, or a western from years ago, Gunsmoke. They keep going year after year, but with a few changes in actors in the starring roles, an abundance of costars, characters, and story lines.

For my first five years or so, beginning in 1945, I can't remember much of the script from that show. People tell me I was there, but the roles I played were small and not really memorable.

After the age of five I became one of the main characters in the story. I had costars like Bob Stein, Gail Dushoff, Jimmy Lovenstein, Mel Strieb, Herb Levin, and Jerry Litvin. And there was my younger brother, Rob, and my older sister, Betsy. The story had cameo appearances by my parents, Louie and Beatrice, a few teachers, Mrs. Barab, Mrs. Clark, Mrs. Oldfield, Ms. Taffee, and Mr. Pass, camp counselors like Steve Seligman and Dave Chapman, and a few pets like Rex, a German Shepard, and a bunch of guppies.

Entering high school began an entirely new "season." I had a fresh cast to work with as many of my friends from earlier episodes went to a different school. New co-stars at Olney High included Larry Stein, Neal Cupersmith, Neal Schwartz, and Tommy Lane. Throughout the show there were cameos by certain teachers: Henry Meyer, Mr. Provenzano, Val Udell, Mrs. Graeff, Don Yonkers, and a lot of different girls.

In the next episode, which took place at Temple University, I again had a new cast to interact with. These costars included a wide range of characters including Ron Shervin, Steve Parness, Louie Lazar, and Jay Seidel in the early part of the opera. Halfway through the season the cast changed. Low ratings, I guess. The new cast included Phil Robinson, Dick Olitsky, Dick Mennan, and the woman I met and eventually married, Terry Del Quadro. Mixed in with the various storylines were cameos of old friends and a few teachers like Jackie Steck, Joe Carter, Delwin Dusenbury, Val Udell and Norm Link.

With the show remaining on the air due to better ratings, the next few seasons included events like getting married, buying a house, having kids, trying different jobs, and starting a business. All of which made for great viewing. Again, the directors brought in a new cast of co-stars including Charley "Rip" Van Winkle, Dick Louderback, Larry Brown, Ted Valliere, Bob Young, John Butterworth, Nancy Noble, Bruce Voss, Andrea Strader, Dan DeSantis, and Ron Zucca. During this period, the show took place in numerous venues including Pennsylvania, Washington, D.C., Utah, Texas, and different sites throughout New Jersey.

Running out of fresh story lines, the show moved to South Carolina for a three-year run. It started with me taking a position at NCR in Columbia, SC, freelancing for several companies and ended with a return to the North. During that time another new cast was brought in to reinvigorate the opera. New costars and repeat characters included Liz Pearson, Eli Cassorla, Freddie Layberger, Mitch Smith, and Steve Lounsberry. There were cameo appearances by my daughter, Laura, as well as other family members.

With filming shut down after the seasons in South Carolina, once again the producers and directors attempted to revive the series by trying a different approach, The Freelancer. Rather than portraying the star as the head of a small production company, he would work from home as a freelance writer and instructional designer. The approach allowed the show's director to keep the co-stars to a minimum and use more cameos, which would reduce production costs. After a slow start, getting used to the new scenarios, the show continued on for another twenty years from 1996 to 2016. Besides the main star there were a few co-stars, mostly cameos. These included Marcy Altimano, Christine Creter, Tim Martin, Lance McGinnis, Jay Oakes, Richard Feldsman, Jean Lambert, Linda Palladino, and four grandchildren, Natalie, Stephen, Amelia, and Will.

As is the case with many long-running shows, to increase audience interest, the episodes began to deal with the personal experiences of the main character rather than specific cases or life-changing situations. The main character appeared to be tiring of the action and sought to go in a new direction to extend the life of the show.

New episodes dealt with retirement and activities that could be incorporated into them, such as gardening, the growing sport of pickleball, and deep-water volleyball played in the pool at the Ocean City Aquatic and Fitness Center. Cameos in these episodes included Marianna Karayiannis, Kate and Roger White, Ward Reese, Bob Swartz, John Kopitsky, Maggie Lundgate, Peg Chernow, and a cast of dozens.

Up to this writing the opera has been going on for over 78 years. Though the main character has a long-term contract for new episodes, how many there will be is to be determined by someone higher up, possibly the president of the network, since he has the power of life and death over this series.

This latest volume, "Yet Another 101 Tales of a Middle-Class Middle-Child" provides more humorous stories and lessons learned by the main character of the series including several based on true-life accounts provided to him by family and friends.

You will also notice a great many names mentioned in this book. This was intentional for several reasons: folks like to see their names in print in a positive way, rather than just in their obituaries. It's also a great way to sell copies.

Chapter 1: A Lifetime of Experiences

I've found that there's a new story worth telling every day. All you have to do is look for it, realize what's going on and scribble down a few notes on a page or into a file. When you're ready to write, take your time, have some fun with it, read it over, and then rewrite it.

The In-Laws

In the film *Meet the Parents* Robert De Niro plays the role of Jack Byrnes, a suspicious father. Jack does everything possible to find out more about his daughter's boyfriend, Greg Focker (Ben Stiller). Greg's first visit to his girlfriend's parents' house turned out to be more nightmarish than he could ever have imagined. My initial and future visits to my future wife's parents' home in South Philadelphia were quite different.

Unlike Jack Byrnes, a retired CIA agent and a Vietnam War veteran who was overprotective of his family, slightly paranoid, and took an instant dislike towards Greg, a middle-class Jewish nurse, my future in-laws, Natalie (Non) and Martin Del Quadro, were friendly to me from the start. I think they were surprised that their daughter, a veteran of a Catholic school education, wanted to go out with a Jewish guy.

That's not to say we didn't have differences as the dating continued and our relationship became more serious. Like Greg, a middle-class Jewish guy, my social and cultural position was juxtaposed against the elder Del Quadro's, especially my future mother-in-law's South Philly Roman Catholics beliefs.

From the first night on, when her parents went upstairs to sleep, I aways thought there was a hole in the ceiling where they could keep an eye on us.

As things got more serious and my presence at their home increased, I met more of their extended family including numerous aunts and uncles, like my wife's Aunt Milly (her given name was Carmella, but nobody ever called her that), who worked for Sears and her husband, Paul Zuest, employed by Sealtest. Paul had actually broken-down the ethnic barrier before me as he was of Irish descent, plus we had the same initials, PZ. On my future mother-in-law's side were the Ciminos of Sicilian decent, Tony, Paul, and Joe, a former president of Teamsters Local 107, along with his wife, Nancy.

My father-in-law also had a large family, including sisters, Angie, Flossie, and Rita, along with brothers Anthony, and Lou, and their extended families. Many of them lived just a few streets away. They all seemed to get along, which was quite different from my father's family.

To put it mildly, my future mother-in-law tolerated me and I her. Her nickname was "Ma Barker." According to her, I would have been perfect for her daughter if I was Catholic. She even cooked me a steak on Good Friday, which even surprised their kitchen. One evening I cracked a joke, which Natalie did not appreciate. In fact, she chased me around the dinner table with a frying pan.

I clearly remember a night when my future bride and I went to a party at her cousin's home in Broomall. As we prepared to leave, an ice storm appeared making driving back to Philly treacherous. Since this was prior to the era of cellphones we had no way of letting her parents know where we were. It took more than 90 minutes of slipping and sliding to reach their home. Her parents were furious by the time we arrived. However, they didn't want me to drive home in that weather and prepared a bed for me on the living room couch.

When Non and Marty decided to take a vacation in the Poconos one summer while we were dating, Terry would not go without me. So, they invited me to come along. I'm sure it wasn't the trip her parents originally planned as I slept in a room with Marty, while Terry roomed with her mother. With today's morals the room arrangements might have been different.

We married in September of 1968. At that time our apartment in Marlton, NJ was not ready, so for several weeks we lived with Terry's parents at their home in South Philly. About a year later, when our first son, Stephen, was born, they met us at the hospital in Philly to take care of our pet rabbit, Fifi, who loved chewing their electrical cords.

A year later, when we purchased our first home in Cinnaminson, NJ, Marty and his brother-in-law, Paul Zuest, rented a truck and moved us with white glove treatment. Terry's parents also bought us a Maytag washer and dryer which we kept for 23 years with no never a need for a repairman.

Once we were married, there were few arguments about religion and we never really talked about politics, though Marty loved Frank Rizzo. He even changed his voter registration to vote for him. Overall, we got along well for many years. Often, Marty would offer me five dollars if I drank a beer. However, I never took him up on it, only because I didn't like the taste.

When Marty passed in 2009 related to a fall from a ladder while picking figs from a tree in their back yard, Natalie moved in with us in Ocean City for more than six years. However, when she began to suffer from dementia and became devoid of reality. She wanted to go back to South Philly to take care of her long-deceased parents, so we had to place her in a nursing home for her own safety.

Looking back on the entire situation, I couldn't have asked for better or nicer in-laws.

The Cappuccino Fix

For Lent, my wife, Terry, gave up her weekly 16 oz. cappuccino which I always purchased for her on Saturday mornings at the local Wawa. With Lent over, I stopped at a Wawa to get her favorite beverage while out picking up a few additional things for Easter dinner at the local supermarket.

Though not my usual Wawa, I stopped at one next to the supermarket to get her the cappuccino. I went into the store, picked up an empty 16 oz. cup and went to the machine for a fill-up. After putting the cup under the appropriate nozzle, I pressed the button for the liquid to dispense. What came out was a very pale colored watery version of the elixir. Knowing this wouldn't do, I put the cup on the side of the dispenser and left the store.

I then got back into my car and drove a mile down 34th street to my regular Wawa. I went in and picked up a 16 oz. cup in the center aisle and went to the machine. When I placed the cup under the nozzle this time I was greeted by a big puff of powered mix. It was followed by the flow of a dark-looking liquid, more closely resembling a traditional cappuccino than flavored water. As is my barrister style, I slowly pushed the button several times, allowing for a good mix of cappuccino and little water to enter the cup. I then covered the drink and got into a line to pay.

There were several people ahead of me, but the line moved quickly until there was only one person ahead of me, a young lady in a plaid skirt, I guess probably in her early thirties. She was purchasing a small coffee, a yogurt, and a small package of cheese and meat. When she went to pay for it with her phone, the cashier told her she didn't have enough money in her account to pay for it. A little startled, she told the cashier that she was parked right outside and would get the needed funds out of her car. I smiled and patiently waited for the transaction to be completed. In the meantime, the line behind me was getting longer.

About a minute later the lady came back and pulled out two dollars. "Oh," she said. "I thought I had a five in my purse." A little frustrated, she told the cashier to cancel the sale. In the meantime, the line to pay was getting longer. Apparently, the cashier was new and had never cancelled a sale and didn't know how to perform the task. A little perplexed, the cashier called the store manager over to help her. The manager, who had been there for years, explained the steps, and then completed the cancellation.

Finally, it was my turn to pay. I pulled out some old-fashioned cash and paid for the cappuccino. In the meantime, the folks in line behind me, unaware of what happened in front of me just gave me a menacing look. Like the delay was my fault?

As the introduction to this chapter points out, there's a new story in one's life every day. All you have to do is look for it, possibly learn something, or hopefully laugh about it.

A Comedy of Errors

Back in the 1960's and 70's famed commentator Walter Cronkite hosted a live program called "You Are There." It featured reenactments of famous events like the death of President Lincoln and the Hindenburg Crash. Cronkite always closed the program with a statement something like this: "What kind of day was it? It was a day like all days filled with those events that alter and illuminate our time, and you were there." I recently had one of those days. And I was there in the middle of it.

It was a Friday morning. I started with my usual Friday routine. I stripped the bed, put the sheets in the wash, did my morning exercises, and ate breakfast. Looking at the time, it was about 8:30. I had about two hours before going to the pool for a game of deepwater volleyball. I figured I had enough time to go to the Lowe's in Egg Harbor Township, about 10 miles away, to exchange a faulty propane tank and pick up a few items we needed. So, off I went.

I made it to Lowe's by 9:00 am, placed the propane tank outside near the propane storage station, and went in to do an exchange. There was a lady at the self-checkout who quickly handled the sale. Usually, you have to wait for a person to unlock the case and provide me with a fresh tank. To my surprise, she told me the case was unlocked and that I should just take a fresh tank. She said they were on the "honor system." My thought was they were understaffed or had cut staffing. In the long run it was a time saver for me.

I placed the fresh tank in my car, secured it so it didn't roll, and went back into the store to get the other two items on my list: a gallon of Mr. Clean, and a large cup hook for our banana holder. The old hook was kind of crusty and needed to be replaced. I found the Mr. Clean right away and then went over to the hardware section of the store. After a little searching, I found where the hooks were located. I had brought along the crusty hook to make certain the replacement would match. As hard as I looked, they didn't have a match, especially with the screw part of the hook.

Figuring I had wasted enough time there, I checked out with the same lady in charge of the self-service section. Looking at my watch, I believed I had enough time to try Home Depot just across the highway for the hook. Long story short, they didn't have a matching one either. So, I headed home, put the sheets in the dryer, changed into my bathing suit and went to the pool.

After an uneventful game of deepwater volleyball, I went home to take a shower, change, and get ready for the cable company which was coming to repair our service between 2 and 4 pm. It was bad enough trying to get a live person on the phone from the cable folks to discuss a problem, but getting someone to actually come out was a luxury, and I didn't want to screw it up. But that's not where this story is going.

When I arrived home from the pool, I took off my wet clothes and prepared to get into the shower. It was a few minutes after noon. Before I could get wet, the phone rang. I saw the call was from a Pennsylvania number and thought I recognized it. I picked up the phone and said, "Hello, Doris," thinking it was our friend, Doris Kemper, who had recently lost her husband, John. She asked for my wife, Terry. I told her she wasn't home. My wife was on her communion run delivering the host to several older residents in town.

Thinking there was a problem, I asked, "How can I help you?" All the time thinking this was Doris. She asked if there was bus service in Ocean City. I told her, "No, but you could always call an Uber or Lyft for a ride." Then, I asked why. She told me she had a doctor's appointment at 1:00, her car was outside, but she wasn't allowed to drive.

This struck me as funny, but it went right over my head. "How did Doris get down here? She lives in PA." I then asked her where the doctor was located. She told me at 6th and Asbury. I immediately knew who the doctor was, but wondered how she was able to get an appointment. However, that didn't seem to matter at the time.

Wanting to be helpful and assist a damsel in distress, especially an old friend, I told her I would pick her up between 12:30 and 12:40 and drop her off at the doctor's office. As for taking the lady back home after the appointment, since I didn't want to miss the cable guys, I figured Terry could manage that.

I then took a quick shower and got dressed. As I was getting ready to leave, my wife returned from her religious run. I told her what was going on and left to pick up Doris – I thought! I drove over to her house at 33rd and Haven. As I pulled in the driveway, I didn't see another car. "How did Doris get here? Did one of her sons or the granddaughters bring her down and leave, or take the car?" My only thought was to get Doris to the doctor for her appointment. As I pulled into the driveway, I beeped the horn and waited. No Doris. I then got out of the car, went up to her door and knocked. No response.

I thought the worst. I pulled out onto the street, beeped again. No response. Worried, I called my wife on my cell and asked her to call Doris. She did. Doris, it seems, was home in Glenn Mills, PA. It wasn't her in the first place. My wife checked the phone number of the call we had received. It wasn't Doris. It was Marty, a member of her bible group. Marty is in her 90's and has dementia. Her children had taken the keys to her car away. Now things began to click in my mind, however late. I headed home.

As I was walking in the house, Terry had her coat on. She had called Marty and told her she would take her to the doctor. Terry took her to the doctor's office. She gave Marty her cell number to call when she was done and then drove home. Terry didn't want to tie up our landline as we were waiting for a call from the cable company.

After finishing her lunch, which was interrupted by the trip to the doctor's office, Terry decided to go back and wait for Marty in person, rather than wait for her call, knowing how forgetful the lady was. Sitting in the waiting area, she heard one of the staff asking Marty where she got her prescriptions filled, as the doctor was ordering two of them. Knowing Marty's condition, Terry joined the conversation. "Look!" she told the admin, "I'm her driver and I'm the person who would have to take them to a pharmacy and get them filled." With a little prodding, Marty said she filled her prescriptions at the local CVS.

With Marty in tow, Terry took the scripts and went directly to the CVS. She handed in the two and explained that she was the driver for Marty and needed the scripts filled right away as she couldn't come back later. The pharmacist filled the scripts in ten minutes as Terry and Marty waited. Luckily, Marty was able to find her credit card to pay for the drugs.

Terry then prepared to take Marty back to her home. As they reached her house, Marty was unable to find her keys. Terry looked in Marty's handbag and couldn't find them either. Figuring Marty may have lost them at the doctor's or CVS, she brought Marty back to our home to call the doctor's office and check with CVS for the keys. In the meantime, the cable company had arrived and were working to resolve our problem.

With no luck in locating the keys at the doctor's office or CVS, Terry contacted Marty's son who had a code to a lockbox at Marty's house which contained a spare key. With the code in hand, Terry took Marty home once again. As she tried entering the code, it didn't work. In the meantime, Marty found her keys in a secret compartment in her handbag and was able to open the door. Terry walked her inside and Marty closed the door when she left.

As for the cable problem, it was squirrels. They had chewed through the sheathing on the cable wires above the house which allowed water to get in and interrupt and downgrade the signal.

A perfect end to a perfect day. As Walter Cronkite said, "What kind of day was it? It was a day like all days filled with those events that alter and illuminate our time, and you were there."

Change of Life

If you're a senior citizen (male or female), you're familiar with the expression "Change of Life." For women it means the onset of menopause, the natural pause of menstruation. When women talk about it, they may say, "I'm going through the change. In men it's a time when certain parts of the body don't work like they used to. I can tell you that is frustrating.

There are also different things that can cause dramatic changes in a person's life beyond natural occurrences in the body. For example, when people are forced out of their normal existences by earthquakes, floods, tornadoes, or war.

I recently went through a change of life experience. It was not as dramatic as those listed above but it has affected my wife and me. I'm talking about home delivery of the daily newspaper. For more than 50 years we had the Philadelphia Inquirer delivered seven days a week. We also had a local publication, The Press of Atlantic City, delivered daily for more than 15 years. Now we get The Inquirer and The Press via the United States Postal Service. It's not that they don't do a good job. The problem is for decades we had the paper delivered first thing in the morning, usually by 7:30 am.

My wife and I enjoyed getting the papers early and reading them over breakfast every day. We didn't mind getting a little printer's ink on our hands, or the chairs, or the kitchen cabinets. It came off. That's how we began our days.

Now, with mail delivery, The Inquirer comes after lunch. Are we supposed to read it over dinner? As for The Press, they're only printing three days a week and we get the Sunday edition on Saturday, The same with The Inquirer. Are they able to predict the news in advance or are they full of "old news?"

Of course, we can get the digital editions of the papers online, but it's not the same. I like to sit at the breakfast table with a cup of tea, my breakfast, and the paper in my hands, not on a cell phone or a computer screen.

I was actually warned about this happening over a year ago by my sister, Betsy, living in Louisiana. She told me The New York Times was no longer going to deliver the paper to her. I thought, "Okay! She's in Lake Charles and that's a long way from New York. I never thought it could happen just 65 miles from Philly and 12 miles from Atlantic City with The Inquirer and The Press.

So much for the question, "What's black and white and read all over?"

A Failure to Communicate

In the previous story, Change of Life, I explained how the lives of my wife, Terry, and me changed due to a change in a routine that had lasted more than 50 years; reading the daily newspaper at breakfast. Though we were notified by the delivery folks about 30 days in advance that our papers would not arrive every morning, we didn't realize the effect until it actually took place. Sure, we could get e-editions in the morning, but it wasn't the same.

However, left out of the notifications were details on how our TV Weekly magazine would be delivered, as it usually came with the Sunday Inquirer.

When the latest copy of the magazine failed to arrive with the Sunday edition, which now arrives on Saturday, I began to speculate that something was amiss. Luckily, I had the phone number of the magazine publisher, due to an earlier delivery problem, and called, as it is no longer listed in the publication.

After navigating through the menu maze, I finally reached a "live" person named Tracy. I explained to her the problem. Apparently, her company had never been notified by The Inquirer that the paper was discontinuing morning delivery by a live person. What caught me by surprise was her mention that they were getting an unusually large number of phone calls. She now knew the reason why.

Thinking back, you would expect that a highly rated and respected publication like The Inquirer would have had its ducks in a row and communicated to the magazine publisher that its delivery mode was changing. But it didn't. What came to mind was the classic line uttered by Strother Martin in the movie *Cool Hand Luke*, "What we've got here is a failure to communicate."

Tracy converted our magazine delivery mode from carrier to the Postal Service. When I asked about getting the current edition of the magazine, she said she would contact someone and try to get someone at the Inquirer to deliver a copy. I wondered about that as they no longer had any delivery people. I chuckled when I heard that. She then added that if we didn't receive a copy in two days to call back. I was hoping I didn't have to.

Two days passed and I didn't receive my copy of the magazine, so I called. This time I wasn't able to reach Tracy. I was forced to go through the entire explanation once more. The man told our subscription was converted to postal delivery. However, I wouldn't be getting my next issue until four weeks later, let alone receiving a copy of the present edition. A little frustrated, I asked to speak to a supervisor. I waited on the phone for 15 minutes then hung up. I tried calling once more. This time, after going through the menu waiting to speak to a live person I was disconnected. I tried one more time but couldn't get any satisfaction.

The Reluctant Volunteer

Over the years I've volunteered my time, energy, and knowledge on numerous endeavors such as coaching different sports teams my children were playing on, umpiring baseball games, working an amusement booth or in the food tent at the carnival where our children went to school, providing guidance and assistance for my high school reunions, and serving as a commissioner for a local sports program. It just seemed like the natural thing to do.

Some of my volunteering was the result of getting things done, not liking the ways things were going, or seeing the need to take charge of a situation.

When I first signed up for the Master Gardener's Program through the Rutgers Extension several years ago, I was "gung-ho." I loved my little vegetable garden in the back yard and enjoyed landscaping our home in Ocean City. Even though the course was several hundred dollars and classes were twenty miles away, I didn't mind the trip once a week because I wanted to improve my gardening knowledge, as folks were always asking me questions about plants. I figured if I took the course, I could answer more of their questions correctly and charge for my answers – just kidding. My advice, good or bad, was and is always free.

Half-way through the 22-week course the COVID-19 pandemic hit. Classes went from "live" in person to online sessions. Three-hour classes in person with a break was a lot better than three hours online with a break. After completing the course and passing the final exam, opportunities for volunteer work were very limited, as the pandemic was still going on.

When the pandemic began to wind down and the restrictions lowered, volunteer activities such as building library gardens, attending town fairs, and visiting farms and local wineries began to appear. However, something changed. Me and my priorities. The "gung-ho" was gone. I was a few years older, my interests had changed, friends were passing, and there were other things I wanted to do. They included writing books like this one, meeting with old friends for lunch, and still engaging in several athletic activities like beach and deepwater volleyball, as well as pickleball. I also found I didn't have the energy I once had. After playing ball I needed a nap. That was about the only thing I could voluntarily do. And now I do it often.

The Best Laid Plans

Ah, the best laid plans of mice and men. How often have you planned something, thought you covered all the possible bases, and then something unexpected happens that throws you for a loop. Take for instance this recent event.

My wife belongs to a bible study group. Every Tuesday morning from September to June they gather at a different member's home to discuss different aspects of the holy book. Many of the members are in their 80's and 90's. Some are unable to drive and require another member or chauffeur to bring them to the session. Although up in years, they still like to gather, chat about what's going on in the town, and then discuss the assigned chapter for the week.

Sad to say, not every member of the group has all their marbles. One participant, Cathy, whose car keys were taken away by her offspring for safety reasons, likes to attend the gatherings. As a result, my wife usually picked her up and brought her to the sessions.

As it turned out, Cathy had a birthday on the day before a recent Tuesday meeting. Wanting Cathy to feel appreciated and loved, my wife asked me to pick up a birthday cake at the supermarket that could be served as the main refreshment at the Tuesday session. At the store I selected a fresh 8-inch round cake decorated with balloons from the case. It had the words Happy Birthday already on it. I then had one of the bakers write Cathy's name on the cake in the same color and brought it home.

Not wanting to give away the surprise of the cake when she picked up the lady the next morning, Terry brought it to the home of the member holding the bible session the night before. She also called the birthday girl to remind her of the meeting and to tell her what time to be ready for the ride.

At the appointed time, my wife arrived at Cathy's home and knocked on the front door several times. After a few minutes, the woman's grandson finally answered the door. My wife asked for Cathy. She appeared a few minutes later in her nightgown. "Oh!" she said. "Is the meeting today? "Yes," my wife responded, I'll wait for you to get dressed." Not wanting to spoil the surprise of the cake, she didn't mention it. After some hemming and hawing, Cathy said, "I think I'll stay home today."

Disappointed, my wife went on to the meeting without the birthday girl. At the session each attendee had a piece of cake, which they told me was delicious. My wife saved a large piece for the missing birthday girl, the part with her name on it. After the meeting she delivered it to Cathy to enjoy. Upon seeing it she replied, "I guess I should have gone to the meeting." My wife just smiled.

Neither Rain, Nor Sleet, Nor Snow

The United States Postal Service, founded by Benjamin Franklin in the 18th century, has a motto. It goes something like this, "Neither rain, nor sleet, no snow will keep our letter carriers from delivering the mail." That may be true. However, I've found that many a customer can make even getting the mail to the carriers a problem.

Here's an example based on a recent experience. When I need to send something via snail mail, I generally stop at the post office in the next township, Marmora. The clerks are friendly, fast, and the facility has an easy-in and easy-out parking lot. However, on this particular day I was in another town, Linwood, dropping off an Amazon return at the UPS store located on Route 9. Since I knew there was a post office nearby, I brought along a small package to send to my daughter, Laura, via priority mail.

Now, the post office in Linwood is a small place. Also, there is no parking in front of the building. You have a choice of either making a right turn on to the street before the building and parking on a side street or parking a block before the facility, where legal parking is allowed. Since I saw an open space on the block before the post office, I pulled in there.

I walked down the street to the facility and entered. I noticed a line of four people in front of me and thought, "This shouldn't take long." My mistake. The first person in line, an older lady, asked for nine priority mail envelopes, "That's easy I thought." Then came the kicker, "Can you give me the postage for the nine envelopes? I want to take the envelopes home, fill, address, and mail them myself." I had never heard of this. When I wanted to send something priority, I picked up an envelope, filled it, addressed it, and sealed it at home. Then took it to the post office, where the clerk checked the address, and printed out the correct postage – a fixed amount.

The courteous clerk, a little taken back, but unfrazzled by the request, told the lady he wasn't sure he had the stamps to fulfill the request, but would try as each envelope if mailed to an address in the United States would cost $9.65. He had to create $9.65 nine times for a total of $86.85. Not an easy task. 10 minutes later, after numerous attempts to meet her needs in the most expeditious way, he succeeded. "That will be $86.85," he said with a smile. Not that the customers behind her were smiling and the line growing longer behind me and out the door into the lobby – As I said it was a small post office. To top it all off after paying and getting a receipt, she said, "Thank you. I guess in the future I'll fill and address the envelopes at home. Then you can just put the exact postage on them electronically."

The story doesn't end there. The next person in line wanted to mail a package to India. Then, the man in front of me had several parcels, as well as one containing lithium batteries which the clerk wouldn't take.

When I finally reached the front of the line, I handed the clerk my small, priority package for my daughter. The clerk looked at it closely. He noticed it was properly sealed and addressed. "Thank you," he said. "You did it right!" He electronically put on the correct postage, and I paid him the flat rate for the item which would arrive in two days and left passing by the now line of 8 people who were behind me.

There are two things I learned from my visit to the Linwood Post Office. The first was to never go there again. The other, which I noticed while waiting, was that there are different sized flat rate priority boxes I had never seen before. Next time I go to my regular postal facility I'll have to ask about them.

Customer Service Gone Askew

I relish talking about customer service. Some companies are great at it. Others stink. Take for instance, a recent letter we received from our gas company. It stated that they didn't have access to our meter for an accurate reading for several months and requested access to read the meter by leaving a key somewhere or providing them with a current reading.

Simple enough, right! We've lived in our present home for more than 20 years. The gas meter is on the outside of the building where it has resided forever. Our house does not have a fence around the area where the meter is located, and the gas company has successfully read it since we have lived here.

Bugged by the letter I attempted to call the gas company to find out what was going on. After going through an endless menu of choices, I finally thought I had reached the customer service center. A voice came on the phone and told me the wait time was six hours and thirty-four minutes. I couldn't believe it. Something had to be wrong. I hung up and then tried again. This time the voice told me the wait time was nine hours and four minutes. Once again. I hung up.

Frustrated but still determined I went on the company's website and found the contact information listed there. Knowing I couldn't get anywhere on the phone, I sent an email asking about the letter. It was never answered.

Two weeks later I received a survey from the gas company asking me to rate their response to my email. Needless to say, there wasn't a rating low enough on their scale.

Thanksgiving Lasagna

Every year at Thanksgiving, like many families in the United States, we have turkey with all the trimmings. We usually get a boneless breast which is easy to cook, cut, and leaves little waste. My wife makes cranberry nut muffins, cooks up delicious mash potatoes, and if my son Dennis' family is coming, she makes string beans.

One year though, things were going to be different. As we were getting older and putting out a big spread became a bit more time consuming and challenging, one of our daughters-in-law, Michelle, volunteered to bring the turkey – she was going to order it from Heavenly Ham; however, she was late trying to order the bird. She was told by the company that people place their orders for Thanksgiving in August to reserve a bird, not two weeks before the holiday.

Unknown to us at the time, and since we qualified for a free turkey, chicken, or other item by spending enough money at the local supermarket and were under the impression that the daughter-in-law was bringing the main entree, we opted for a frozen, family-sized vegetable lasagna. Not that I would eat it, but it was for our granddaughter, Natalie, and her fiancé, Nick, who have different palettes.

When notified of the problem with the Heavenly bird, I purchased two boneless breasts to feed all the meat eaters. However, we still had the frozen vegetable lasagna. Estimating how much the granddaughter and her fiancé could consume, we realized it would be waste to defrost and cook the entire lasagna. We decided to cut the frozen slab in two, cook one half of it, and put the other half back in the freezer for later consumption.

That's when the fun began. We started with a large, sharp knife. That didn't even dent the slab. After trying every blade in our kitchen armamentarium, we looked for another approach. In the garage, I found a sharp Stanley handsaw used for fine cuts. With my wife holding the lasagna upright and I cutting away on the kitchen countertop, we split the slab in two. What a sight. If only there were a picture or video capturing the event. But there were only two of us.

When we finally separated the lasagna, we looked at each other and laughed. We smiled and swore, "Never again!"

The Cemetery Run

I've heard of beer runs, food runs, and bathroom runs. However, when we were first married, I wasn't familiar with the Catholic tradition of what I call "The Cemetery Run," going to the different cemeteries where family members were interred and placing grave blankets in front of the tombstones.

My first introduction to this practice came while having morning coffee with a fellow named Rocky Stefano when we lived in Cinnaminson, NJ. Just before Christmas, Rocky would tell me he was making "The Cemetery Run" that day which included trips to three different cemeteries in Pennsylvania where his wife's parents and relatives were buried and placing grave blankets on them. In the Jewish tradition, during any visit, we would just place a small rock on the tombstone of the family member(s) buried there to let them know they were not forgotten.

While my father-in-law, Marty Del Quadro, was alive and able, he would take my mother-in-law, Natalie, on the sojourn to St. Peter & Paul Cemetery in Springfield, Delaware County before Christmas. Once at the grave site they placed the blankets with bows on the graves of her parents and her brother, Tony, and his wife, Rose. When Marty passed the tradition fell upon us to continue it.

A couple of weeks before Christmas, my wife would purchase several fresh wreaths at Produce Junction and decorate them with bows. Her handiwork turned them into attractive grave coverings. We planned our cemetery run based on weather conditions. Cold was fine. Snow or rain in the forecast was a "no go." We also tried to time the trip to miss rush hour traffic or Eagles' home games.

Living in Ocean City, the cemetery run was a bit longer than traveling from Philadelphia. Often, starting out on a Sunday morning at about 9:00 proved to be the best option, weather and traffic permitting. From our house to the cemetery was a distance of 84.2 miles. The route included the Garden State Parkway to the Atlantic City Expressway, Route 42, going over the Walt Whitman Bridge, taking Interstate 95 south to the Blue Route. From there we would take Exit 5 on to Sproul Road, making a left into the cemetery and then finding the graves, which was always fun if you can have fun in a cemetery.

Although we had the section and lot numbers for the graves, finding them was often a challenge. Some were covered with pinecones and straw, and if there was snow on the ground it was almost impossible. In fact, though we knew the general area, we sometimes passed right by the graves. A Marine flag marker for my father-in-law helped to narrow our search.

Once we found the graves, which were all in a row near a large pine tree, we placed the decorated blankets in position and used metal wires to secure them in place. The entire trip up took about 90 minutes. But it was high speed and often white-knuckle driving. Something we are not used to doing these days.

With the initial task complete, we had one other stop to make at the cemetery. Another of my wife's relatives, her Uncle Paul, was buried in another part of the cemetery. From past visits we had a general idea where the grave was located. Also, his gravestone was a different color than many of the others. Without too much trouble we located it and placed a wreath there. Our task was complete. Unlike my friend Rocky, we only had one place to visit, rather than three.

After positioning the last wreath, we looked at each other and smiled. We had completed the run for another year. All that remained was safely getting back home.

Let's Do Lunch

How many times have you said to a friend or colleague, "Let's do lunch!" and it never or seldom happens. However, in retirement I try to make it a reality. For years I would meet with an old friend from high school, Larry Stein, in Hammonton, NJ.

Larry lived in Southampton, near Mt. Holly, New Jersey. Hammonton, New Jersey, the Blueberry Capital of the world was a half-way point. Larry would come south, down Route 206 to Route 30, the White Horse Pike. Located on a corner at that intersection is the Silver Coin Diner, a grand old-fashioned eatery with a large menu, great food, excellent burgers by the way, and scrumptious desserts that make your mouth water in anticipation.

When Larry moved to the middle of nowhere in Virginia, our lunches stopped because halfway was now somewhere in the middle of Maryland, hundreds of miles away.

Luckily, I still have several other friends who are willing to meet me at The Silver Coin as it was about halfway between where they live and my home in Ocean City. On almost a monthly basis, I'll meet with a fellow named Joel Toussaint. I've known Joel for over 40 years. He attended St. Bonaventure in upper New York state. We used to play volleyball on Wednesday nights and also got together for lunch at the Prospector in Mt. Laurel, New Jersey when he was working for ARI, a car leasing company based in that area. Now residing in Belmar, his trip to the diner is about the same distance as mine. When we get together, the first discussion is usually about health, his and mine, what's happening in our lives, and who died. One thing we never discuss is politics.

Another friend who is usually willing to make the trip to The Silver Coin is Nate Rosenblatt. Nate lives in Cherry Hill and at this writing is still working at the age of 80. He doesn't know what else to do. We first met almost 50 years ago when he was working for a magazine publishing company in Philadelphia. His firm needed someone to produce advertising presentations for the company's different products and I got the job.

Our lunch conversations often begin in the same way as those with Joel, concerns about health, his and mine, what's happening in our lives as well as those of our families. We also reminisce about old times, some of the zany projects we worked on together, as well as the nutty folks we worked with. Between Nate and I political discussions are on the table as we have similar thoughts in that arena.

Besides having a great lunch, no trip to Hammonton and The Silver Coin would be complete without a stop at Bagliani's Market in Hammonton. Located on the main drag, this Italian themed establishment is one of my favorite stops for quality prepared foods, cheeses, cold cuts, Angus beef hot dogs, fresh Federal Baking Company pretzels, and a super selection of breads and rolls.

Another reason I like going to Hammonton is the price of gas. The stations in Hammonton are usually about ten cents per gallon cheaper than the Ocean City area. Actually, there's only one gas station in Ocean City.

In the end, I must admit, I'll go almost anywhere within an hour's traveling time for a good lunch and conversation. In the past I've met folks for lunch in Bordentown, NJ, at Mastori's Diner, which is now closed, The Cracker Barrel – numerous locations, and The Pub on the airport circle in Camden, NJ. Good conversation, good friends and good food are worth their weight in gold. When you have all three the end result is priceless.

Never call me Sneezy

Remember the dwarfs from the story of Snow White? Today calling a person a dwarf isn't politically correct. However, in folklore or fantasy literature, when the story was originally created, dwarfs were considered members of a mythical race of small, stocky humanlike creatures who were generally skilled in mining and metalworking.

In Snow White, there were seven of these folks: Doc, Happy, Grumpy, Sleepy, Dopey, Bashful and Sneezy. Though I'm not dwarf-sized, I could have a nickname at different times similar to most of them, like Happy, Grumpy, Sleepy, and Dopey. For example, after a winning game of pickleball you could call me Happy. After a loss, you might call me Grumpy. After swimming or pickleball Sleepy may be an appropriate title. And if I make a stupid mistake, you could call me Dopey. However, depending upon the time of the year, like spring and fall, I could easily be called Sneezy.

Here's why. Ever since we moved out of Philadelphia and into suburbia in 1970, I have suffered from allergies. This was not the first time. In the 1950's, while attending summer camp out in the country near Collegeville, PA, I would get headaches from time to time due to what was blowing around in the air.

Living in suburbia turned out to be a challenge. In the spring and fall I'd start sneezing like crazy. Plus, there was congestion, sore throats, and sinus headaches. Numerous attempts to handle the problem with over-the counter remedies and magical concoctions failed. Even Alka Seltzer tablets didn't help. As a result, I decided to get tested for my allergies in the hope of resolving the problem.

In those days, testing involved a scratch test across the upper back. The doctor would subcutaneously inject different liquid allergens like dust mites, mold, a variety of trees, and animal dander. Based on the test results, my physician had a custom serum created to help control those things I was most allergic to, which included dust and some trees.

For over 40 years, from doctor to doctor, as we moved around the country, I was able to receive a once-a-month injection. I'd pay for a year's supply of the serum from the manufacturer which they would send to my physician's office. That was until a couple of years ago.

The Run Around

When I went for my shot in January of 2020, the nurse practitioner said I needed a refill. So, while I was there, she faxed the refill information to the laboratory.

Knowing it usually took about four weeks to formulate and ship the new serum, I let things ride for a month. After 30 days I called the company billing me for the serum over the last several years. It turns out they said they had no record of the prescription or my account. I gave them my doctor's name and number. Long story short my doctor again faxed over the reorder form.

Having been unsuccessful in my attempts to get the magic serum, I called the company again and was given the lab's direct number. I couldn't get a live person. All I could hear was a faint, difficult to understand voice. After two attempts at a translation, I called customer service. They suggested I contact the company's pharmacy department by selecting Option 3, which I did. Once again, I was told they had no record of my prescription. I gave the customer rep, Carole, my doctor's phone number. She said she would contact them and also gave me a different fax number which I gave to my physician's office.

Two days later I again called the pharmacy department. They said had no record of the doctor's refill order. By now I was flipping out. But I held my temper and gave the person the doctor's number one more time. She said she would call my doctor and then call me back.

Long story short, she never called me back. Adding insult to injury, after my 2-month wait I learned that the prescription would only be refilled if my doctor opened an account with the laboratory. The doctor really didn't want to do so because he wasn't an allergist. He was only administering the monthly injections as a courtesy to me. This I understood.

So, here I was 2 months without my serum, and since we had a mild winter, my allergies were acting up. No fun! I started to think I was really Sneezy.

A Blessing in Disguise
Stuck between a rock and a hard place, I called my primary care physician's office for advice. They recommended two local allergists. After reviewing each of their credentials and patient comments online, I made an appointment with one.

Of course, the earliest appointment I could get was three weeks away.

Battling sneezes, headaches, and a runny nose for several weeks, the day finally arrived. When I walked in, I was given 5 pages of forms to fill out. You know the drill these days. The one question I really loved was "Why did you stop your allergy shots?" My answer – It was not my choice.

After completing the paperwork and forking over my copay, I was ushered into an examination room where a friendly nurse, Sarah, reviewed the paperwork and asked me a few additional questions. Several minutes later Dr. Schwartz came in. We discussed why I was there and what his approach to my case would be. He felt I didn't need a full-blown workup. He recommended a less invasive one, and it could be done immediately in the office.

Within a few minutes the nurse, Sarah, returned with vials of allergens. She wiped down my forearms with alcohol and proceeded to place 28 marks on them with a black sharpie. Then, she proceeded to subcutaneously apply an allergen to each mark. When she was done, I was told not to scratch any itches and that she would be back in 10 minutes. She returned, examined the eruptions on my forearms, and documented the results for the doctor.

A few minutes later another nurse entered and told me the doc wanted to do an additional 13 pricks on my upper arm. This time I was told to wait 20 minutes. After 20 minutes a timer went off outside the room. Then another nurse came.

She examined my arm and recorded the results and told me the doctor would be in shortly.

Several minutes later Dr. Schwartz came in and we discussed the results. Apparently, no major culprits revealed themselves. The tests showed I was allergic to dust mites, mold, and also dogs. Many people are allergic to mites and mold, but we didn't have a dog.

Choices

Based on the test results I had two choices. The first was to have the doctor create a custom serum and I could begin weekly injections. The second was to forgo the shots for the present time and use a strong antihistamine when I had a headache. If I chose to begin the shots at a later time, the allergist had all the information needed to develop a serum.

Since I had gone several months without the serum with only minor discomfort, I decided to try the "no shot" approach for several months. In the meantime, the allergist prescribed a strong antihistamine which was covered by my insurance.

Thinking about it now, after all the trials and tribulations of trying to get my original serum, and having a new scratch test, maybe it was a blessing in disguise. In terms of dollars and sense, it saved me a bunch as I was paying for the serum. And it was getting more expensive every year. On top of that there was the charge for the monthly injections.

It's been several years since my last shot and I'm no worse off than before. The only thing I miss are the monthly interactions with the friendly personnel at my primary doctor's office. Now, I only go for a yearly wellness check or if I'm really under the weather.

There's Always Entenmann's

I don't know about you, but during the week I normally sit down to a wholesome breakfast on Monday, Wednesday, and Friday mornings. The meal usually consists of a fresh banana, a red delicious apple, two pieces of whole wheat toast, and a cup of decaffeinated tea. When playing pickleball on Tuesday and Thursday mornings, I substitute a bowl of Apple Cinnamon Cheerios for the tea and toast. However, when the weekend arrives, I go a little wild and crave a tasty donut or two.

Over the years I've had a great range of donut choices, depending upon where we are residing. Back in the 1970's, when we lived in Cinnaminson, NJ, there was the Chestnut Hill Bakery, just a few streets from our house. The bakery featured a wide assortment of those delicious delicacies including glazed, chocolate-filled, chocolate-covered, powdered, vanilla-covered, and jelly donuts.

When that bakery closed for some reason (it couldn't have been from a lack of our business) I was forced to make a longer run on to the L&M Bakery in Riverside, NJ, about 20 minutes away. L&M has been around for many years and makes great donuts, as well as out of this world pies and cakes. There's usually a line on weekends, but it's worth the wait. In fact, now, twenty plus years later, when he's in the mood during the summer, one of my sons, Dennis, will stop there on a weekend and bring a dozen of those dangerous treats to us in Ocean City.

When we were living in South Carolina, the best donut to be had was at Krispy Kreme. When the red light in the window of the store was flashing, hot glazed donuts were flowing down the product line, and you could never eat just one. Sometimes they offered a free one with a cup of coffee. However, after that you needed to purchase a second, third on an entire dozen. They were addictive.

At one time there actually was a Krispy Kreme store in Northfield, New Jersey, not too far from us. For some reason it closed and is now a shoe store. No, they don't give you a donut when you purchase a pair of shoes.

Living in Ocean City for more than 20 years I've had an opportunity to sample the offerings of a wide range of donut sellers, especially during the summer months as many bakeries in the city close after the first week in October.

While bike riding on the boardwalk one Saturday morning in June, I saw a line of folks at the northern end of the boardwalk. They were at an establishment known as Brown's and waiting for donuts. They were selling freshly fried donuts with an assortment of toppings. Being what was known as a Brown Virgin – never having sampled their products, I purchased a half dozen. Though many people swear by them, Brown's just wasn't one of my favorites.

During those summer months, one of my favorite places for donuts is Dots. They have a great assortment of tasty offerings including round glazed, pretzel shaped glazed, jelly, powered, and cream filled, chocolate and vanilla covered and twists. All fresh and tasty. But you'd better get there early as the line is usually out the door. They've also gotten a lot more expensive.

If I'm in the mood for cake donuts I like Mallon's at 14th and Bay. Primarily known for their cinnamon buns and crumb cake, their assortment is enough to please any cake donut aficionado.

After Columbus Day (or Indigenous People's Day), early in October, most of the fresh bakeries close. As year-round residents we are left with fewer choices. Those include individually wrapped donuts provided at the local Wawa. The store selection often includes chocolate covered, chocolate filled, vanilla covered, and old fashioned glazed, if you get there early. In my opinion, they're okay in a pinch if you really need a donut fix.

As for those baked treats at the supermarket, I've found them to be pretty heavy. And of course, there's always a Dunkin around. However, I've found that if you buy them on Saturday and they're not finished, they're usually hard by Sunday. Of course, if all else fails you can always buy a box of Entenmann's chocolate covered ones.

Supermarket Friends

I do the food shopping for my family on a regular basis. What I've learned is that if you go to the same supermarket week after week, year after year, it's important to make friends with the people who work there. If you have a "friend" in the business, it's almost as good as having a relative there, not that it will get you a discount.

At my local supermarket in Marmora, New Jersey, I've made friends with more than a half dozen folks who work there. It's more than just smiling at them. A short chat pays dividends in the long term.

My friends at the store include Anthony, a rather tall fellow in his early seventies. Anthony stacks the shelves in the personal care area that includes vitamins, body lotions and creams, toothpaste, and a wide range of OTC items. He always has a smile on his face and will assist you in finding an item you can't readily locate on the shelves. He's even gone across the store to locate an item for me which was not stocked in his area.

Another stacker I'm friends with at the store is Lou, a short balding fellow of about seventy. Lou grew up in Philly and graduated from Frankford High School. Lou is a talker and chatterer. He's also a diehard Eagles fan, especially when they're winning. He's happy when he bets on them or covers the spread and wins. Plus, he's always open to hearing a good joke.

In addition to Anthony and Lou there's Sue, a personal shopper, who knows where almost every item in the store is located. She's a petite lady with her hair always pulled back in a ponytail and wearing a Shoprite blouse with her nametag. You can't miss her. Sue can often be found picking up items for six or eight customers at a time. Many a time she's assisted me in locating an item, especially after the store has rearranged the shelves. Why do they do that?

One of my favorite departments in the store is the meat department managed by a lady named Pat. Besides saying "hello" when we pass each other, Pat helps me select a great tasting spiral ham at Easter, as well as a great filet roast at Christmas. Working several days a week with Pat, is my neighbor from across the alley, Dave. If you don't see a cut of meat you like in the case, Dave will cut one for you.

Once I've filled my cart based on my list for the week, I head towards the checkout area. If the lines aren't too long, I'll head in the direction of one of my favorite cashiers, either Cathy, Gail, or Mary Ellen. Mary Ellen is usually at the first live checkout. She's always polite and cheerful and willing to help you bag your purchases. It turns out that she graduated from the same high school in Philly as my wife, Saint Maria Goretti located in South Philadelphia.

The second cashier I'll seek out is Cathy. For some reason I thought she looked like a Bernadette to me. At least that's what I called her until I read the tag on her sweater. Cathy is a petite lady and works there to keep busy after her husband passed. If neither Mary Ellen or Cathy are available I'll go to Gail. I guess she's in her middle 50's and is always ready to lend a hand packaging up your groceries.

The other person at the store I've gotten to know is Sandy at the Customer Service counter. If I have a problem with an item, such as if I was overcharged by the computer system or didn't receive credit for a digital coupon, she's the lady who will handle the problem and make things right.

Having supermarket friends is almost as good as the new theory of relativity – "Having a relative in the business."

The Make-Up Bouquet

For years I've done my supermarket shopping on Monday mornings. At that time of day, the store is generally less crowded, and the workers have or are in the process of restocking the shelves from the maddening weekend rush, especially during the summer.

On one particular Monday, early in July, I parked my car in the lot, grabbed my list and reusable shopping bags, and headed toward the store to purchase our groceries for the coming week. After selecting a smooth and clean rolling cart (one with a recent oil change and lube) from the stock outside, I walked in and moved to the right to set up my cart for the task ahead. I usually accomplish this by laying out the weekly circular across the "child" seat and place my shopping list and any product coupons on top of it. Unlike my wife, I like to stick to the items on the list. I'm not an impulse shopper.

I always start my shopping in the fresh baked bread aisle, pick up some steak or brioche hamburger rolls, and also check out any tasty-looking treats like an apple or cherry pie to satisfy my sweet cravings. Opposite the fresh baked area in the store is the floral department.

Since I had been involved in an unwinnable argument with my wife earlier that morning, I thought a fresh bouquet of flowers might be a great peace offering. Carol, the manager of the department, was putting out some fresh floral arrangements that had just arrived. I asked her if she could suggest a nice "make-up" bouquet. She said, "I have just the thing." Carol then pulled out a beautiful and vibrant bouquet of colorful flowers from a box she was emptying. "Wow!" I thought. "Terry would really like that." Though it wasn't on my list, I believed it would be well worth the investment. As it turned out, more than I would have known. I thanked Carol for her help and laid the bouquet carefully across the child seat in my cart and continued my shopping.

From the floral department I moved on to the fresh fruits and vegetables picking up several red delicious apples, a bunch of bananas, and some baking potatoes. These were all things on my list. Up and down the aisles I went picking up a package of 85/15 Angus ground beef, mild pork sausage, and Bob Evans mashed potatoes. Along the way, several "supermarket friends," Lou, a shelf stacker, and Sue, a personal shopper, said "Hello," and commented on the beautiful bouquet on the top of my cart. I remember Lou saying, "What did you do to need to buy those flowers?" I just smiled and went about completing the day's list.

My journey up and down the many aisles in the store continued until I reached the packaged bread department located in the last aisle of the supermarket. If white or whole wheat bread is on my list, I always check the expiration date on the package to make sure the product is fresh for at least another week. I generally purchase Sara Lee or Pepperidge Farm if they have good dates.

It was there that the real adventure began. After checking the color-coded dates on several loaves of Pepperidge Farm Whole Grain bread, and selecting the freshest one, I turned to put the loaf in my cart. To my surprise the cart, loaded with my flowers, groceries, and bags was gone. I was startled. At first, I wondered if one of my "supermarket friends" was playing a joke on me, but none of them were in sight.

I looked back up the bread aisle for my cart. It wasn't there. Aisle by aisle I retraced my steps across the store, from the soda and water aisle, up and down the paper goods aisle, through the frozen foods section, past the cleaning products and detergents. But my cart was nowhere to be found. Undeterred I continued my search for it all across the store. I began to wonder if I couldn't find it, would I have to start my shopping trip all over? What about the bouquet?

As I reached the first aisle at the front of the store, where I had started about 30 minutes earlier, I saw my cart. It was being pushed by an old man about five feet six, wearing a Phillies baseball cap, T-shirt, and thick glasses.

I could tell the cart was mine from the make-up bouquet of beautiful flowers Carol had helped me select for my wife. The bouquet was the only one like it in the floral department. And there it was lying across the child seat where I had placed it, along with my shopping bags, as well as my selection of groceries in the cart. On top of the flowers were several items that I knew weren't mine. I took a minute to consider what I should do to reclaim my cart and decided a direct approach would be the best.

Holding my loaf of Pepperidge Farm bread in one hand, I went up to the older shopper and politely said, "Excuse me, sir, but I think you have my shopping cart." Startled, the man said, "Yours?" "Yes," I said. "These are the flowers I selected for my wife. And in this cart are my groceries, and my shopping bags. Are these things on your list?" As I pointed to the Angus ground beef and Bob Evans Mash potatoes.

The slightly confused and upset man looked at me and said, "If this is your cart, where's mine?" I replied, "I don't really know where you left it in the store. Maybe it's in the bread aisle where you took my cart. These are my flowers, bags, and groceries. Can't you tell?"

Adjusting his glasses, he looked closely at the cart and realized he had made a mistake. He took the few items he had laid on top of my make-up bouquet and went on his own cart-hunting expedition across the store. Happy that I had recovered my cart, I put the fresh loaf of bread in it and went to the self-checkout with everything on my list plus the make-up bouquet.

When I arrived home, I handed my wife the bouquet. She smiled at me and said, "Thank you. The flowers are beautiful, but you're still wrong."

The Unexpected Thank You

As I mentioned at the beginning of this chapter there's a

new story worth telling every day. You never know when one will present itself.

On the Monday morning after my granddaughter's wedding, I took the suit I wore to the affair to the dry cleaners. I was told the suit would be ready any time on Friday. When Friday arrived, after a few other errands, I went to the cleaners to pick up the suit.

After pulling into the parking lot, I noticed a car parking next to me. I thought nothing of it. I didn't recognize the driver. I got out and went into the store to pay for and retrieve my suit. The guy who parked next to me followed me in.

As I went to pay for my suit, the driver approached and said, "Thank you!" I looked at him, a bit surprised. He then replied, "I saw you pull into the cleaners. It reminded me that my wife had wanted me to pick up several dresses she had dropped off there earlier in the week. So, thanks again. I would have completely forgotten about them."

Mr. Fixit Goes to Arizona

As a child growing up in the 1950's and 60's, I remember watching episodes of a TV show called Mr. Fixit. It demonstrated basic home repairs and construction techniques. You could call it an early version of This Old House, not to be mistaken for Home Improvement and the tool man, Tim Taylor.

Being a homeowner as well as a do-it-yourselfer, I learned, sometimes the hard way, that it's important to know how to fix things and also to understand your limits – when to call for professional help for big electrical and plumbing problems. It also pays to think MacGyver when all else fails.

When we started going to Sun City, Arizona on a yearly basis to visit my wife's Aunt Milly and Uncle Paul, who had retired there, I was often called on to play Mr. Fixit and MacGyver at the same time. Take for example a hole in the wall. It seems Aunt Milly wanted the thermostat control physically lowered in the hallway of their home so she could reach it. This was because her husband, Paul, suffering from dementia would always lower the temperature which gave her the chills. She was always cold and couldn't reach the controls. After an argument with the heating company, they agreed to physically lower the control at no charge. However, they left the hole in the wall where it had been. Covering it with just a painting wasn't the way to go.

Not trying to make a mountain out of a molehill and with few tools and materials available in the house, I was tasked with finding a solution. After a thorough search, the only things I could find in the house were some wooden paint stirring sticks in the garage. I broke several of the sticks into pieces and used them to fill the hole. I then went to the local Lowe's and purchased a small container of spackling compound which I used to cover the hole. I then smoothed the surface with sandpaper which I obtained from a nearby dollar store and matched the paint for the wall, as close as possible, using color strips from Lowe's. It didn't pay to buy a gallon, so I just purchased a sample jar which was more than enough to do the job. It wasn't perfect, but it was a great improvement over the hole.

One other needed repair was to a wooden shutter that had been damaged near the front double doors to the house. The opening spring mechanism on one door had broken over time due to lack of use and the Arizona heat. When the door was opened, it hit the wooden shutters and broke a slat. I managed to reassemble the broken slat and applied super glue to hold it together. I then planned to place a small pot with a cactus plant between the door and the shutter in order to prevent the door from opening all the way and wrecking my repair. Of course, after reassembling the shutter, and before I could put the pot in place, my wife opened the door all the way to see how I was progressing and shattered my work. I then redid the project with the pot in position.

A Million Ways to Die in Arizona

In the comic western, *A Million Ways to Die in the West*, directed by Seth MacFarlane, a cowardly sheep herder, Albert, faces a gunfighter named Clinch Leatherwood (Liam Neeson) in a battle for survival. In the end, Seth shoots Clinch in the arm. Clinch, only wounded, laughs. However, it turns out the bullet that struck him was soaked in snake venom and causes Clinch to die.

There were so many ways to die in the old west. It could have been from disease, thirst, heat, Indians, wild animals, rattle snakes, and so on. Today, there are many other ways to meet your maker while out west. On various trips to

Arizona, we faced numerous challenges that could have easily left us planted on Boot Hill from one cause or another.

Here's the story. When my wife's Aunt Milly and Uncle Paul retired to Sun City Arizona in the late 1970's, they planned ahead and purchased space for their final resting places at a mausoleum a few miles of their new home.

Over the next several decades members of the family visited them yearly, including my wife, our three children, Stephen, Dennis, and Laura, as well as my in-laws, Natalie and Marty Del Quadro who even drove out there one time by car.

Taking a week off from work, I made my first trip to Sun City in the early 2000's. The first night we stayed at the home of the aunt and uncle, the fan in our bedroom started to smoke. I began to wonder if after so many years of being married to their niece, they wanted to get rid of me. What a way to go!

On subsequent trips to Arizona, not wanting to end up on Boot Hill too soon, we stayed at nearby hotels. The first year it was the Hampton Inn in Glendale-Peoria, just 20 minutes from their home. It was June and the temperature stayed at 114 degrees, even at night. Another way to go – heat stroke.

After that we came in the fall, when it was cooler, and stayed at an older Day's Hotel, only 10 minutes from their home. It wasn't great, but since it was prime rental time for snowbirds from the Midwest there were no other lodgings available in the immediate area.

As the aunt and uncle aged, our trips to Sun City became more frequent. We made repairs, did landscaping, and helped prepare their taxes. We got so familiar with the area that I was able to give people directions when they became lost. Each year we visited we could see the aunt getting weaker, and the uncle suffering more from dementia. Soon our trips included visits to several assisted living facilities in the Sun City area, but the aunt, who still had all her marbles, made no commitments.

Aunt Milly passed early in January of 2019. The day after we learned of her passing, Terry and I hopped on a plane and made the trip from New Jersey to Sun City to handle her funeral. Luckily, she had found a place for her husband, Paul, to live just a few weeks before she died. Since he was suffering from dementia it fell upon us to make final arrangements for her funeral. In fact, we were informed by his doctor not to tell him that his wife had passed.

Our funeral sojourn was only for a week as my wife was having eye surgery later in the month. Following the surgery and when she was cleared to fly, we returned to Arizona to put the aunt and uncle's home on the market and to get their affairs in order.

On that trip we arrived in the dark and it was raining. Yes, rain in Arizona. We picked up a car at the rental area and started out for the hotel in Sun City. On the way, we couldn't understand why cars heading towards us were flashing their lights. When someone pulled up next to us, they told us the headlights weren't on. In Jersey, cars, if set on automatic lighting, the lights go on when it's dark or when you turn on the windshield wipers. Another opportunity to be planted on Boot Hill in Arizona passed.

On our next trip, after my wife's surgery, we arrived in Arizona for an extended stay of 16 nights and paid for a first-floor room with two queen-size beds. The hotel only had two floors and you could park your car outside your room.

We spent little time in the room, as we had a number of things to accomplish. The list included getting the house on the market, returning cable equipment, making arrangements for an estate sale, paying for the uncle's funeral in advance (It's tax deductible if paid in advance) meeting with the aunt and uncle's financial planner, as well as closing certain bank accounts.

Near the end of our mission, we were awakened one morning at 6:30 am by the roar of a loud motor and the smell of carbon monoxide fumes filling the room. A guest had backed in his diesel truck in front of our room. The truck engine ran for 30 minutes before he left. He repeated his actions the next morning before leaving the hotel grounds. Two more attempts on the lives of the northerners? Two more attempts to get us buried on Boot Hill. This was beginning to feel like the plot of a B movie, and we were the main characters.

Long story short, my wife's Uncle Paul passed about a year later, during the height of the pandemic. Luckily, we had made all his funeral arrangements in advance since we could not get there. It seems the wife of a patient forced her way into the nursing home where he was living and spread COVID-19 to many of the patients. He caught it and never recovered.

Chapter 2: Astute Observations

It's always important to stay aware of what's going on around you. After decades of listening and watching, I think I'm now capable of pointing out some of the things I have observed over a lifetime of trials and errors. Though I know from experience that you can't tell younger generations anything, this is my attempt. I certainly hope someone gets it.

Lucky Me

At this writing I've lived 78 years. I've been lucky. Many of my friends from childhood and later in life have passed due to accidents, illness, disease, natural causes, or just plain old age. I've got most of my original body parts, though they don't all work as well as they used to. But I'll try to continue on.

Why am I lucky? I still have my health. I'm not as fast as I used to be. However, I can still play pickleball, deepwater volleyball, as well as beach volleyball, so long as one of my sons helps me up when I go down to save a ball.

Why am I lucky? I'm still married after 54 years. My wife puts up with me and my quirks, and I with hers. We often think the same thoughts about a person or an event and blurt it out at the same time.

I'm lucky because our children are almost normal. Just kidding. They are normal within certain bounds. When I traveled around New Jersey doing programs about children with disabilities in the 1970's, I realized how lucky I was. Our offspring are all married. Some have kids. Some have cats. Some have both. They each own their own homes and have successful careers.

Why am I lucky? I live in America. With all its problems and bickering, it's still one of the best places to live on Earth. I wonder where I'd be if my grandparents had stayed in Eastern Europe around Ukraine. Would I have even been born. Lucky me.

Why am I lucky? I live near the ocean. Sure, after I'm gone, the Atlantic may eventually reclaim my land, but I'll be long gone, so I wouldn't worry about it. It's something I can't change.

May the spirit be with you.

In many of the Star Wars films, you hear the expression, "May the force be with you." Not being part of the Lucasfilm universe, I don't think it is with me. But something is. Have you ever had the feeling that there's someone or something in the room with you, but you can't see it. You thought you saw it or something while quickly glancing around the room, but then it was gone? I often wonder if I have a guardian angel or in my case several looking out for me.

Thinking back across my lifetime there were a number of times I've been saved, or something occurred unexpectedly that prevented me from harm or helped me excel. One of the earliest events I can remember was when I was about eight years old. Running like kids often do, I tripped near the top of the steep wooden back steps outside our row home in Philadelphia. Below, was nothing but concrete. Somehow a metal trashcan lid was at the bottom of the steps. My head landed on it rather than the concrete. That saved my life.

When I was 13 and studying for my bar mitzvah, I just couldn't get it. I didn't want to do it anyway. However, some force allowed me to memorize my part of the Torah in Hebrew. After the service that ability disappeared.

In high school, I couldn't make heads or tails of algebra or geometry. On my first go round with both, I failed. I failed algebra so bad they wouldn't let me take it over in summer school. I did pass the second time around. However, I then flunked geometry. After taking it in summer school, I aced the second semester of it, aced algebra 3 and 4, without ever taking algebra 2 (due to a mix up by the powers that be) and also aced trigonometry. Strange but true.

On a weekend canoe ride, while in college, my wallet containing my driver's license and other personal information fell out of my shorts in the water. I didn't realize it until we were about to leave. Somehow, I saw the sun shining on the wallet made of elephant hide floating in the lake and was able to retrieve it.

When we moved to Cinnaminson, NJ I joined a men's softball league. One time, while at bat, I hit a ball so far, you would have thought Babe Ruth was at the plate. It only happened once. I think the spirits were having fun with me.

When I was working in the audiovisual field, I produced synchronized slide/sound presentations. On one occasion, I synced up a show that only worked for me. When others tried to show it, it went out of synch.

How about winning a new car at a yearly Catholic carnival where our kids went to school? What are the odds?

While writing another story for this book about an experience where I faced unexpected competition from a former professor who was using his students to complete projects for him, the file went crazy. It was like the spirit was saying to me, "You don't need this one in the book. It sounds like you're complaining." I finally was able to close the file. The next morning, I deleted it from my story list.

A similar experience occurred while writing another tale about getting charged interest from a department store and how I called the company to dispute it. As I went to save the piece it disappeared. Again, the spirit was telling me this one wasn't good enough to make it into the book.

From time to time, I still have a feeling that there's someone or something else in the room with me, but just can't see them. One day I hope to catch a glimpse of them.

A Direct Line to the Almighty

My wife is religious. I truly believe she inherited a religious gene from her mother, Natalie. Terry faithfully goes to Mass six days a week, belongs to a bible study group, and delivers holy communion several times a week to folks in their 90's who are unable to attend church in person. She also belongs to a religious group called the Companions, and aids Sister Joelle, the Director of Elementary Faith Formation at her parish, in any way she can.

Recently, my wife received a call from a friend, Lucia, who lives in New England. Lucia comes to Ocean City for several weeks during the summer. She called Terry to ask her to pray for her daughter's friend who teaches at the Berkley School of Music in Boston. It seems the friend has diabetes and was about to lose several toes due to her worsening condition. She also feared she might lose her leg due to the disease.

Lucia called my wife, because she was the only practicing Catholic she knew and believed my wife, because of her many religious activities, might have a direct line to the Almighty. If anyone had a chance to gain the Lord's ear and help this woman, it was Terry.

When Dreams May Come

In the musical, *Joseph, and the Amazing Technicolor Dreamcoat*, based on Joseph in the Book of Genesis, the hero interprets the dreams of two fellow prisoners. According to Joseph's interpretation, one, the pharaoh's bottler would be set free. The other, a baker, would be sentenced to death. I have dreams too, but no one to explain them to me. Hopefully, one of them doesn't foretell my ultimate demise.

I don't dream every night, but when I do some are very realistic. Others are traumatizing and scare me. In my most athletic dream I was playing touch football, a favorite sport of my youth. In this dream I was a tight end. According to the play called by the quarterback I was going out for a short pass. My task was stop and buttonhook – turn around. The play started. I turned around to catch the pass and found myself on the floor. Yes! I did catch the pass. At least I thought I did. However, the ball wasn't in my hands when I woke up. And my wife didn't have a challenge flag to dispute the catch. She just laughed at me lying there when I told her what happened.

One night I dreamed I was crossing a bridge on a bright sunny day. When I got to the other side, I could see farmers picking strawberries and a fruit stand selling bright red watermelons, but I didn't have any money to purchase them. Who carries money into a dream? I then decided to go back over the bridge and wondered how I would eventually get home. The next morning, when I awoke, my legs felt like I had walked several miles. Go figure!

In other dreams I'm on a plane spinning out of control or I'm constantly wandering around a city after a client meeting, although I've been retired for several years. Several times in dreams I appear lost and can't find my car. I say to myself, "I thought I parked it there on the street," which I can see perfectly, but it's gone. I wonder how I'm going to get home. "Do I take the bus? Do I have exact change? I know I don't want to take the subway, especially if the city turns out to be Philadelphia."

If someone is chasing me in a rare nightmare, I'm lucky enough to realize where I am (in a dream) and wake myself up. Hopefully the culprit didn't follow me into the bedroom. However, I do look around just to be sure. I guess I've watched too many science fiction movies during my lifetime.

A Guide to Napping

The older you become, naps play an increasingly important role in your life. I still remember as a child in kindergarten taking a nap. At summer camp, after lunch we would take 30-minute naps – at least we were supposed to. Of course, the greatest napper of all was Rip Van Winkle, whose nap lasted twenty years. I did at one time know a "Rip" Van Winkle. His real name was Charlie, and I wished he had slept for 20 years.

The second greatest napper that I knew personally was G. Russ Waite, a neighbor for many years. Russ was an expert at it. He could nap almost anytime, anywhere.

As I've grown older, I've learned the value of short ones, and the problems with long ones. After I've played my limit of pickleball games on Tuesday and Thursday mornings, had a shower and lunch, a short nap of 15-30 minutes in my favorite recliner is a great rejuvenator. I'm then ready for the remaining challenges of the day. The same is true on Mondays, Wednesdays, and Fridays after a game of deep-water volleyball at the Ocean City Aquatic and Fitness Center.

However, if my nap runs long, like an hour or even longer, I'm messed up for the rest of the day, as well as when attempting to catch a good night's sleep. I often wake up from my long nap a little groggy and don't feel like doing much. Then, at my usual bedtime, right after 11:00 pm, I'm tossing and turning, and never really get to REM (Rapid Eye Movement) sleep. If I do manage to fall asleep, it's only for a few hours, especially when nature calls. And then trying to get back to sleep is almost an impossibility.

I guess it all goes back to the idea of moderation as you age. Anything, like fine food, exercise, and even a short nap is good, but overdoing it can really mess you up.

Anticipation or a Tailwind?

Here's an interesting phenomenon. Maybe you have had the same feeling at one time or another? When we take a non-stop, cross-country flight west, say to Phoenix, Arizona it can take six and a half hours. However, the return trip is often an hour shorter. Why? Because of a tailwind. That's over a distance of several thousand miles.

But consider this. When we decide to have a meal at a nearby restaurant, like Dino's Diner in Seaville, it seems like forever to get there. Is it anticipation of a good meal or hunger anxiety? From our home we turn on to Bay Avenue, make a right onto 34th street, then a left on Route 9 and go down to the traffic light at Route 50. We then make a right turn on to Route 50 at the Shell gas station. The restaurant is on the right about 200 yards from where we turned. The overall trip is about 9 miles.

The drive to Dino's is generally about 20 minutes or so, depending upon traffic. We pass several banks, drug stores, businesses, housing developments, and even some open space. However, on the return trip, after the meal, it seems like we're home in less than 15, not that I'm speeding. It's the same mileage down to the diner and back. Strange! A tailwind?

Everything Has Its Place

Though folks think I have an amazing memory for things past, that cannot be said of the present. When I'm working on a home project with a saw, hammer, screwdriver, or drill, if I've completed the task or just finished for the day, I make certain I put the tool back in its rightful place, be it a certain drawer, the garage, or our storage closet (for us it's actually a bathtub with shelving located on the first floor). In that way I know where to find it for the next undertaking.

That's important because these days I can walk through a doorway into another room and forget why I'm there. Of course, there could be some hints. In the kitchen it could be for some food or drink. In a bedroom closet it could be for a certain piece of clothing. I guess the only place I'm really sure that I need to do something is when I enter the bathroom. It's either to take a shower, brush my teeth, or shave. With those possible actions eliminated I only have two other choices.

Go Figure

I still like to read the newspaper in the morning at breakfast – a real paper and ink version that I can put in my hands. When we receive an invoice with a price increase for the subscription, I'll often call to negotiate a better deal. Many of those calls were successful while others provided interesting and sometimes mindboggling results.

My first experience with newspapers began as a child. I remember going to Al's on the corner of 69th and Ogontz Avenues daily and purchasing the Evening Bulletin for my father. The cost of the daily paper was five cents. The Philadelphia Inquirer (Inky) was the same price. The thick Sunday editions of both papers were full of comics, a variety of supplements, a colorful magazine, and cost twenty-five cents.

The Bulletin eventually went out of business. When I moved into my own home, I had the Inky delivered to our door. Of course, the price for the paper continued to rise. When we moved to Ocean City in 2001, I still had it delivered seven days a week. We also added daily delivery of the Press of Atlantic City, as my wife was teaching at Holy Spirit High School and wanted to read about the kids at her school and their successes in sporting events, like crew and football.

These days, when I receive an invoice from the Inquirer for 8 weeks, I check the date I'm paid up to. When the "paid through date" changed from the previous invoice I used to wonder why. Then, I called customer service to learn why. It turns out that special supplements like puzzles, food, or sports magazines that sometimes come with the paper affect the price and length of my subscription. I can understand that. I just didn't know about it.

While I'm on the phone with a live person, I'll often ask if I can get a better price for my subscription. Since most papers don't want to lose you as a subscriber, they'll find a deal for you. On one occasion, I mentioned how friends received offers for an 8-week subscription for only one dollar. I was told that was for new subscribers only. However, the rep said she would see what she could do. By the end of the call, I managed to get another twenty dollars off of my 13-week subscription.

While the price for the Inquirer subscription had been relatively stable, that was not true of The Press. It was a smaller paper and became more expensive than the Inky on a 7-day a week basis. And The Press was unwilling to negotiate price.

Sometime after my wife retired from Holy Spirit, we agreed that getting The Press on a daily basis was no longer a priority or cost effective. So, I called customer service to get a price for just the Sunday edition. I was given a price of $65.00 for 13 weeks.

Just by chance, I asked how much it would be for the Sunday edition and one other day of the week, like Wednesday. The representative told me $46.00 for thirteen weeks. I said, "Are you sure?" "Yes!" replied the rep. "That doesn't seem right," I said. "No! That's what it is." replied the rep. I said, "Okay! I'll take it. Give me The Press on Wednesday and Sunday for 13 weeks at the $46.00 price." Go figure!

An Introduction to Politics

Learning is a lifelong experience. Quite often you learn more after graduating than while in school, especially regarding how the world works or is supposed to. Take politics for instance. It seems like politics are all around us, whether we like it or not. If I want to keep friends, I keep politics off the table.

My first introduction to politics came from an unlikely place. After I received my master's degree from Temple University, I stayed involved in the educational media program by taking additional courses. At the same time, I inadvertently became involved in a political battle between the head of the department, Dr. Roger Gordon, and Mary Renner. Mary ran the audiovisual department at the Upper Darby School District just outside of Philadelphia. She was known around Pennsylvania for her support and the advancement of educational innovation.

The professional audiovisual organization in Pennsylvania at the time was the Pennsylvania Learning Resources Association (PLRA). Unknown to me as a new member of the group was a battle for control of the organization between Dr. Gordon and Mary Renner, who had been in the organization for years. My first knowledge of Mary Renner was given to me by Dr. Gordon. He was not a fan of Mary. That soon changed as I began to work with her.

My active involvement in the political battle came when I looked at the publication distributed by the PLRA. From my knowledge of journalism, the newsletter didn't look professional. Knowing it could be improved and also to elevate the image of the organization, my wife and I volunteered to edit and produce the newsletter.

As a result of our involvement, I met Mary Renner in person. She seemed very nice and not a threat to anyone. She was straight forward and to the point. As a result of our working relationship, we were friends for many years.

During our time as editors of the newsletter, my wife and I tried to keep the relationship between Dr. Gordon and Mary Renner on an even kneel. When a question about content arose, we asked for opinions from both before deciding and often presented a compromise of their views as we understood them.

Neighbors and Politics

If you live in a town, a city, on a farm, or even in an apartment house, you generally have neighbors. How long they stay, their ages, distance, family members, friendships and politics will often determine how well you know and get along with them.

Take for instance the first next-door neighbors I ever knew on Georgian Road in Philadelphia. It was the Weiss family, an older couple and their two daughters, Sylvia and Julie. How old was the couple? I'm not sure. Everyone looks old to kids. Our row homes shared the same front steps. I was too young to discuss politics. All I knew was that Mr. Weiss liked to garden.

On the other side of us lived Al and Miriam Lavin. Al operated a shoe store in Easton, PA. I went there a few times in my youth. The Lavins had a son named Burt who went on to become a dentist. He was a lot older than me. Our rear porches were connected, and we shared a set of steps in the back with them. They hung one of my first landscapes over their piano in their front room. They allowed us to plant a vegetable garden on the small plot we shared. I buried many a goldfish and pet turtle there. When Al passed, Miriam moved away within a year. I never really got to know the next family that moved in.

Living next to the Lavin family and sharing the same front steps, was the Wenger clan. Their family unit included a mother and father and two daughters, Julie, the oldest, and Ricki Sue. She was a year older than me. Talk about a small world, I became friends with their nephew, Robert in Junior high. He went on to become a doctor. I remember bowling several times with Al Lavin and Mr. Wenger. When he died, they also moved away. Again, being much younger and having different interests than the adults I interacted with, we never discussed politics.

When I got married, we moved to New Jersey. For the first year or so of our marriage, we lived at the Allison Apartments in Marlton, just off Route 70. Our neighbor next door was Mrs. Mulholland. She was a lot older than us. My wife often took her to church on Saturdays. As a young couple we never talked about politics with her. In the apartment complex we formed friendships with couples our own age, but discussions mostly concerned getting things fixed, where to shop, and who was having a baby and when. The closest we ever got to a discussion of politics was when I lost my job when the funding for it was cut due to a change in federal administrations.

After our first son, Stephen, was born we moved into a house in Cinnaminson, New Jersey. It was a five-year old, three-bedroom, split level. Living there for twenty-three years we knew our neighbors pretty well, or as well as we wanted to. Many of our neighbors had children whose ages were similar to ours. There was Steve and Carol Lutz on one side with their two girls. Carol and Russ Waite and their four boys lived on the other side. Next to the Waite family, on the corner, were Helen and Joe Lehman with their brood. Directly across the street from us lived Gert and Leo Tedeschi and their two boys. Just up the street on Ardleigh Road were the Bernativicus family. They had two boys, Albert and Edward. Their boys were the same ages as our sons, Steve and Denny.

We also were friends with Georgia and Bob Monday. They didn't have kids, but we got along great with them. We were also friendly with the local mayor, Dave Stahl, as I coached several of his sons in soccer. Nobody really talked politics or asked what yours were. It just wasn't a popular topic.

In 1993, we moved from Cinnaminson New Jersey to Lexington County, just outside Columbia, South Carolina. We didn't make many friends there. People were friendly to you on the surface, but you never got invited into their homes. The only neighbor friend we really had was Buddy, a good old boy, who lived across the street. To our neighbors we were Yankees. Politics, let alone anything else, never became part of a discussion.

After three years in the South, we returned to South Jersey. We moved into a townhouse in Delran. Though we resided there for five years, joined by our son, Dennis, we didn't make any close friends as people were moving in and out all the time. We would say "hello," but that was pretty much it. Politics never became part of the hello.

In the infamous year of 2001, we moved to Spruce Road in Ocean City on a full-time basis. Our next-door neighbors at the time included an older couple, the Orios on one side, and Jim Naplasic and his wife, Sharon, on the other side. They had two boys, Jimmy, and Owen. Though we talked about many things, like gardening, beach volleyball (Jim was an avid player) and what was happening around town, national politics or political affiliations were never topics of discussion.

Thinking back about it, we never had discussions with either family about politics. In Ocean City, if you were a resident, you voted for the person, not the party. Political party was never a real problem although this is a very Republican town.

Today, on our particular block, we have weekenders and locals, which makes for an interesting mix. Take the Anders for example, Carol and Frank, a couple in their seventies. They live in Blue Bell, PA and come mostly on weekends, along with their little dog, Ellie, a Lhasa apso, which I call the walking mop. Whenever the little dog sees me, she comes running and wants to be noticed and petted. She never asks me about my politics.

Carol and Frank are nice folks. Carol is a former home economics teacher. She is heavily into gardening and often asks my advice since I completed a Master Gardeners program several years ago. Carol also bakes a mean zucchini bread and often hands out loaves to the neighbors. Frank is rather tall and thin. He describes himself as an executive electrician. He is self-trained and handled many jobs over his lifetime from grunt to assistant manager. On dry mornings throughout the year, you'll often find Frank circling the area on his bike checking out the neighborhood. We never really discuss politics while on or off his bike.

Just down from the Anders live Bernadette and Matt Bechta, along with their Burma doodle, Arnie. Bernadette and Matt are relative newcomers to the neighborhood. Bernie actually grew up a few blocks from me in West Oak Lane, while Matt was raised in the northeast part of Philly. Both

Bernie and Matt like to exercise. Matt likes golf and often plays with his sons. I introduced Matt to pickleball and told him the only way to get better, like golf, is to play. We talk about the old neighborhood and growing up in Philly. We never discuss politics. Whatever the discussion, Arnie is never interested and just lays there politely.

At the present time, our neighbors directly to the right of our home are David and Josephine (Josie) Schwartz. Like Terry and I, she's Catholic and he's Jewish. What are the odds in Ocean City? Josie is a former nutritionist and dietician. She was raised in New York. Dave, on the other hand, grew up in Cheltenham, PA, just a few blocks from my old neighborhood of West Oak Lane.

Dave runs a sunglass business and has several stores on boardwalks and other locations around New Jersey. A third member of the Schwartz family is Bella, a golden doodle, who lets every dog that passes know she is there. Josie and Dave are the third family to be our next-door neighbors. Maybe it's us? They love to take Bella for a daily constitutional every morning. We never discuss politics with Josie, Dave, or Bella.

Our neighbors on the other side are Caroline and Steve Carchedi. They are primary weekenders and presently live in Upper Gwynedd, PA. They purchased their home from the mayor of Ocean City and have made it into a showplace. Caroline enjoys cutting the grass while Steve putters around always looking for new projects to tackle from sheds to a gazebo for his grill. Steve and I get along well as long as we don't discuss politics.

Practical Gifts

Our family celebrates Christmas. My wife loves the holiday, You can tell by the number of containers in the attic labeled "Christmas." She goes all out with decorations, lights, and of course bakes a ton of cookies.

When it comes to gifts for our three children, all grownups, we differ. Terry will give them cash, in addition to beach tags, undergarments, or clothing as well as scented toiletries for the lady spouses. When it comes to my gifts for them, I've been going in a different direction for the last few years. I believe in practical gifts. I know money is practical, but these are gifts that keep on giving.

One year it was a multi-purpose emergency tool for their cars. The compact tool, only eight inches in length, featured a flashlight with different light strengths, a glass breaker, pen knife, small scissors, bottle opener, Phillips head screwdriver, and mini wrench, plus the tool came in different colors.

Another Christmas, I gave them a bag of useful items from Harbor Freight, my favorite "toy" store. Each bag included a pair of scissors, a magnetic parts holder – you know how small nuts and screws fly all over the place when you take something apart. There were also several tubes of super glue, a paint brush, and clamps – great for when you need to hold something together as glue hardens. My gift also included a set of funnels, and a pair of safety glasses. The little things that are great to have even though you never thought of them until they were needed.

Recently, I hit the jackpot with two practical gifts for each child and their families. One was a battery-powered, LED shop light, which was much brighter than a traditional flashlight. The light also came with a hook you could use to hang it almost anywhere. At the time I was buying them it was "buy one get one free." With three kids and me that made four.

The second and most popular item among all the gifts for everyone was a Battery Daddy. It holds more than 100 batteries, including AA, AAA, 9-volt, C, D, and those circular lithium ones. One family went out the next day and purchased enough batteries to fill the case. You can never have enough batteries, especially when the smoke detector starts beeping every three minutes at 3:00 am and indicates the battery needs replacing. Battery Daddy to the rescue.

Better than Murder and Mayhem

Being raised on television from the 1950's I had the opportunity to watch and enjoy numerous sitcoms. Many are still viewable on channels like Antenna TV and TV Land. Some of my favorites included *Happy Days*, *Barney Miller*, and the original *Night Court*.

Each week, for 11 years, from 1974 on we looked forward to watching a new episode of *Happy Days*. Set in the 1950s and 1960s in Milwaukee, the sitcom told the story of the Cunningham family -- Howard, the father who owned a hardware store, Marion, the stay-at-home mom, their son

Richie, and their daughter Joanie. With each show we learned more about the family and their friends.

What trouble would Richie Cunningham and his friends, Ralph Malph and Potsie Webber get into? How would Arthur "The Fonz" Fonzarelli, the local bad boy who filled his days with fixing cars and dating girls, bail them out? We were amazed at what the "Fonz" could do with the snap of his fingers or a tap on the juke box at Arnold's Diner.

Year after year we watched as Richie grew up, dated, and joined the U.S. Army. It was simple fun with little real drama. The show was one you could watch as a family and enjoy. *Happy Days* launched many spinoffs, including *Laverne and Shirley*, *Mork & Mindy*, *Joanie loves Chachi*, as well as others.

These days, when I'm tired of watching murder and mayhem taking place on police dramas like *Law and Order*, *Chicago P.D.*, and *CSI* and want some humor, I turn to *Barney Miller* reruns. The series, which ran from 1975 to 1982, focused on the lives of the detectives in New York's City's12th Precinct station house in Greenwich Village.

The early episodes looked at Capt. Barney Miller and his work and home life, but the show gradually concentrated more on the detectives of the precinct, including the always-on-the-verge-of-retirement Phil Fish, as well as Nick Yemana, Stan Wojiehowitz, Ron Harris, and Carl Levitt who always wanted to become a detective.

Occasional visits from Capt. Frank Lugar, Lieutenant Ben Scanlon the bitter and recurring nemesis from NYPD

Internal affairs, and Arthur Ripner, the shyster lawyer always looking for new clients, just added to the laughter. You can often recognize several young Hollywood stars who made initial TV appearances on the show as criminals. Though the show lost several cast members after its first few seasons and added new detectives, it's still fun to watch.

The original *Night Court* was also great. The show focused on the night shift of the Manhattan municipal court. The series centered around the court's eccentric staff, wacky court cases, and the endlessly hilarious legal practices of Judge Harry T. Stone, a young, hip, jeans-wearing liberal eccentric presiding over the night shift -- which meant his views on various cases were not always normal, nor his judgments. Helping him manage the chaos was the not-so-bright yet softhearted courtroom guard Bull and an egotistical prosecutor Dan Fielding, played by John Larroquette.

One memorable, recurring character on the show was John Astin, as Buddy Ryan. He was Harry's eccentric biological father and a former mental patient. His catchphrase to stories involving his hospital stay was "...but I'm feeling *much better* now." It was always accompanied by a huge lee ring grin. The show was a critical success. In my mind, the latest rendition of the show doesn't measure up to the original.

Commercial after Commercial after Commercial

While I'm on the subject of television, as a writer, I enjoy watching a good, creative TV commercial. However, today there just seems to be way too many of them on the regular and cable channels.

In the 1950's and 60's I was used to seeing one to three commercials every fifteen minutes. Now you get 7 to 10 every 10 minutes. The programs are shorter by several minutes and the commercials more numerous. Just the other day I watched an old show on a streaming channel since I had missed its regular viewing time. It had no commercials and ended almost 8 minutes earlier than on regular TV. If you watch the local evening news, the broadcasts end at least three minutes earlier than the scheduled time. Those 3 minutes are filled with at least 6 or more commercials.

What about the content of these promotional productions? In the early days of TV there were a ton of cigarette commercials: Winston, Camels, and Lucky Strike to name a few. I loved the western music with the Marlboro Man, but he died of cancer.

Since smoking is banned because the FDA finally decided it caused cancer we are treated to a bevy of commercials for cars, car and home insurance, and drugs. Some insurance commercials I find humorous, like those for GEICO, NJM, and State Farm. While others are annoying like Progressive's Flo and her crew, or All State and Mr. Mayhem who is always destroying something. I dislike them so much; I won't buy their products even if it would save me a few bucks.

My reactions are probably typical because they are based on tested theories about commercials. The entire strategy is focused on the idea of remembering the product being promoted. I enjoy watching a good spot and hopefully will remember the product. The same could be said about a bad commercial. You hate watching it and still remember the product, and perhaps buy it.

How about drug commercials? There are a host of them promoting different medications for treating cancer, diabetes, heart failure, kidney disease, and more. If you listen carefully to the side effects presented by the voice over printed in the fine print at the bottom of the screen, you have to wonder if these possible effects are worth the risk. The idea here is to ask your physician about the medicine. I have!

What about the plausibility of commercials? At Christmas time you'll see a couple standing in a snow-covered field. The young, handsome guy tells his wife, "I bought you something." He whistles and a St. Bernard pup comes running towards them. The wife picks up the pup, holds it, and then says, "I bought you something, too." Next thing we see is a bright new pickup truck rolling into view that he stands next to and hugs. What we don't see is her handing him the coupon book for the monthly payments.

I also get a kick out of the spots for a certain paper towel product. Something spills, like juice or tea, and it's flowing towards a winning lottery ticket, rug, or an iPad. Why don't they just pick up the ticket or the computer and move the object out of the way? Wouldn't it be simpler?

Here's another thing. I know the truly ideal utopian world has no prejudice in it and maybe advertisers are trying to help bring that about. But how many mixed racial families are there in this country? Do so many commercials have to illustrate it? Some examples you've probably seen include a recent holiday BMW commercial or DISH TV promos.

One of my pet peeves is fast-food company commercials, especially for burgers and chicken sandwiches. Is the chicken breast that large that it sticks out of the roll? Not where I go. Do the burgers look that good when you get them at Mickey D's or BK? Not the ones near me.

What about the words in fine print on many car commercials "Do not attempt this" or "Vehicle on a closed course," where the vehicles are climbing steps, doing wheelies, or situated on an impossibly high cliff. It could only get there via helicopter.

No discussion of commercials could be complete without a mention of those late-night advertisements on cable. You know, the ones that tell you, "Just wait!" and they offer you a second product like night vision glasses, super bright flashlights, or wide-angle rear-view mirrors for free, just pay a separate fee. They never tell you what the separate fee is? Why don't they just tell you its additional shipping and handling charges. That's the new legalese way of saying it. And, if you read the fine print on the screen, it tells you they will offer you other products when you call or go online to order.

I also get a kick out those commercials that tell you they're stopping production of the product or that there are supply chain problems, and you can only order two. Maybe they should have never made the product in the first place.

Save $$$$s When You Switch

I also love the ads on television for car insurance. They often say, "Switch to us and save an average of $500 to $700." I even get advertisements in the mail telling me the same thing, especially when they know my policy is almost up. How do they know that?

Don't you wish that you could really save several hundred dollars by switching and receive the same coverage? We live in New Jersey and the rates are really high for full coverage, but I wouldn't want to be without it.

Consumer Reports suggests that you check out other companies every few years to see whether or not you're getting a good or fair shake.

I recently took CR's suggestion and checked out several other well-known companies to compare rates. You can do this over the phone or online since companies know everything about you, except the name of your mistress (If you are lucky!).

What I found was interesting. One well-known company, with no jingle or mascot, was actually higher than what I was paying for our two cars. My current policy offered breakdown insurance for up to seven years. This other company's agent wasn't even aware of this benefit because they didn't offer it. He said he would tell his daughter about it as she had just purchased a car.

Another well-known company that sent me a letter and also advertises on TV became part of my survey. They too offered rates higher than what I was presently paying. The only way they could be comparable was if I switched my homeowner's policy also. Of course, when you live east of the Garden State Parkway, it's no bargain.

One other company I checked out could save us about $100. However, I hate their commercials so much I wouldn't switch.

Serengeti Superior

Online shopping makes things easier. At least it's supposed to. There are some things I generally won't buy online like food, shoes, and clothing. Inanimate objects like batteries, simple devices, print cartridges, and cleaning products generally are not a problem. But nobody's perfect. Especially not a big online operation like Serengeti Superior. That's not their real name, but you know who I mean.

What gets me are some of the things Serengeti tries to get away with. Take for instance a recent purchase of a Christmas tree stand. We had the same plastic stand for more than five years. It held water and provided a way for us to straighten the tree once it was placed in the stand. After five years of good service, it cracked as plastic often does over time. Not wanting to take the chance that it might leak and ruin the floor, I decided to replace it.

With a little research on what was available and checking a ton of reviews, we decided on a sturdy stand made in Germany. It was available in several sizes, small, medium, large, and extra-large. Based on the height of the tree we usually buy at Christmas, I selected the medium. Serengeti had it at about the same price as other online sites. But since Superior offered free shipping, that seemed the way to go. So, I ordered it.

A few days later it arrived in a box that looked like it had been through a war. The box was torn. You could see where there had been a previous shipping label adhered to it. One of the pieces that is used to adjust the tree was sticking out of the box. The whole thing appeared used. Nowhere on the website did it say we were buying a used stand. We sent it back and were given a gift card for the amount, not a real credit.

Here's another example. We have a Simple Human trash container in the kitchen. It uses a G size bag. Purchasing replacement bags in the brick-and-mortar stores was expensive. Serengeti had a good price for a box of Simple Human brand G bags in a quantity of 100. I ordered a box. What arrived was a pack of 20, not 100. I waited a few days to see if the other 80 would show up. They didn't. Trying to figure out what happened, I called customer service and explained the problem. I was told to keep the 20 and they would send me a box of 100.

Two days later another pack of 20 bags was sitting in the mailbox. Again, I waited a couple of days for the missing 80. When none arrived, I called once more and went through the same explanation. This time they told me to keep the 20 bags I had received and order another brand of G-sized bags on their site. When I went back to the site, the Simple Human G bags in a quantity of 100 were no longer available. However, I did find another company offering G-sized bags in a quantity of 100. They were cheaper than the Simple Humans I wanted and just a tad smaller. Long story short they work, but they were not the ones I wanted.

Serengeti surprised us on another occasion. We had crown molding installed in our great room. When the carpenter got to the cold air return vent, he partially covered it. When the original cover was put back, you could see drywall through the cover. The reduced return vent was an odd size. However, I located one on Serengeti available at a fair price. So, naturally I ordered it.

When the cover arrived, I noticed it had a slight bend. There was also a note saying, "Thank you for giving this slightly used item new life." Nowhere on the website did I ever see a description stating that it was used. I guess that's why it was so inexpensive. Also, after the purchase, that size was no longer listed. Unable to find another, I used it. Once it was screwed into place, I'm the only one aware of the slight bend. Who looks at cold air return vents anyway? But that's not the point.

The Jump Start

Just like a well-traveled battery may require a "jump" to get your car going on a cold morning, I do the same for my body on a daily basis. Since I'm past the age of 75, I follow a strict regimen of exercise every morning. It's a great way to get my body moving. Even though I may not have had a good night's sleep or have a few aches and pains I stick to it.

The jump start allows me to get through the remainder of the day which may include pickleball two days a week, and deep-water volleyball three days. During the summer I add beach volleyball on Saturday and Sunday. The secret is to follow the routine, no matter what, no matter how you feel.

The first part of my charging process involves a series of lumbar exercises. I somehow make my way to the floor in front of our bed with a towel and a small pillow. The towel is for my head. It keeps the carpet clean as I go through my workouts. The pillow is for my calves when I get to my ankle exercises.

Once on the floor face down, I begin with the Cat Back Stretch, which I repeat 10 times. I follow that with the Cobra Stretch, again 10 times. I then roll over on my back and complete 10 repetitions of the Leg Cross-Over exercise. Next, it's back on my stomach for the Bird Dog. This time holding each leg in position for 2 minutes. Then, for one last time, I'm on my back again completing some Abdominal Bracing, followed by 25 half sit-ups, and finally 12 ankles circles for each leg, with my legs supported by the pillow.

I then somehow get up off the floor, stand up and stretch out my body against a door. Next, I stand on my toes for 12 repetitions. The entire jump start takes about 20 minutes to complete.

After finishing the toe stand, I hop in the shower, and with warm water running down my back, I slowly massage my lower back for about two minutes before washing down the rest of my body.

Once I've dried off, I apply Wood Lock, an old Chinese remedy to my lower back, and rub in a small amount of Voltaren® Gel on both knees, and some on my right ankle. Then I'm ready to go.

After engaging in the sport of the day, pool volleyball or pickleball, I will take another shower and give my lower back another brief massage. Once dried off I apply some ZIMs Max freeze to my lower back. Then, I'm ready to tackle my daily chores or take a nap.

(You can find the specific details for the different lumbar spine conditioning exercise programs on a variety of ortho websites.)

The Magic Number

Everyone needs a few rules to live by. It could be how you greet people, what to wear and when, taking meds, or in my case athletic endeavors. There is one rule I follow faithfully although it changes with age. Simply stated, "When you get to the age of 75 stop playing the game when you reach your magic number."

The magic number for beach volleyball is 3 games at a time or in a row, and don't play if there are fewer than five members on your team. With deepwater volleyball, the time limit is 45 minutes. It doesn't matter how many players there are on each team. You're treading water, not swimming the English Channel.

With pickleball, it is stopping after a maximum of four or five games. Of course, that can depend on how long each game runs. Some can be quick, others may take up to 25 minutes, depending upon who your partner is and the competition.

As much as I enjoy these different sports, which I'm still happy to be playing or at least standing on the court at over 75, I stop when I hit that magic number.

Often folks will ask me why I'm stopping or leaving. I simply tell them that I've learned to listen to my body. After the succession of games in either sport, my body tells me, "I'm tired and it's time to stop." Even though the brain may say it's okay to continue. Stopping allows me to come back and play again on another day. Continuing, especially when you're tired, is a setup for injury.

If I'm able to continue without embarrassing myself or having a serious injury the magic number could change.

What constitutes a blueberry muffin?

Every Saturday morning, I travel to the local convenience store to purchase that cappuccino fix for my wife. Occasionally, I'll have an urge for a blueberry muffin that the store carries. They're just over two dollars each and don't taste too bad. However, when I get home, I cut the muffin in half, butter the insides, and heat it up in the microwave.

There lies the problem. How many blueberries make a good muffin? Generally, I count the blueberries I can see when I split the muffin. More often than not there are only a few of these antioxidants visible in the entire concoction.

Does having only 3 berries in a muffin really allow you to call the muffin a blueberry? It reminds me of the nut who sued Subway for calling their sandwiches Footlongs when they were only 11-inches in length, only in reverse. Or the restaurant advertising Hasenpfeffer (rabbit stew), when it only has one rabbit in the pot and the remainder in the pot is horse meat.

You Bet Your Life

Do you remember the great Groucho Marx? He was generally considered to have been a master of quick wit and one of America's greatest comedians. He and his brothers, Harpo and Chico, did slapstick comedy in films for years, like *A Night at the Opera, Duck Feathers, Horse Feathers,* and *A Day at the Opera.*

After his film career, Groucho, with his signature mustache and large cigar, hosted a TV quiz show called *You Bet Your Life.* During the show, contestants working in pairs answered questions for money. If they were unable to provide the correct answers, Groucho always gave them a final question that was hard to get wrong such as, "Who's buried in Grant's tomb." That way no contestant went home without winning something. There's a new version of the show featuring Jay Leno, but he's no Groucho.

The point of my little intro is to call attention to some of the latest advertisers on TV, which involve opportunities for folks to bet on sporting events and play casino games online. Every day there seems to be a new one popping up: FanDuel, PointsBet, BETMGM, WynnBet, DraftKings, Caesars to name a few. The ads, among others, feature a sexy young woman dancing on the golf course, a bowler throwing a gutter ball and being happy with his result, or a guy playing Caesar in full costume. I'm sure you're familiar with many of these.

Today, you can bet on almost anything: who will win the game, which team will score first, how many points will be scored in a quarter or game, how many shots a player will take, how many he/she will make, who will hit a home run. It pervades every professional sport.

When it comes to cards and games of chance the online casinos will offer first time bettors their money back in different amounts up to $1000, or points where winners can cash in later. Then, in small print, it states that if you have a gambling problem, call this number for help. I know for some people gambling is an addiction. It's like getting hooked on alcohol or heroin. In some ways, like drugs, it can literally kill you or destroy your family by losing your home. How many people say to themselves, "I can win! Just one more bet." That's all it takes. In some cases, with that first uncontrolled attempt, you are literally betting your life.

Although we live less than a 30-minute drive from Atlantic City and its casinos, we seldom visit. At one time, when my wife was teaching, the school Christmas party was held at one of the casinos. It included a wonderful buffet with great food and dancing. At the end of the event, we would wander into the slot machine parlor, convert twenty dollars into quarters and have a go at it. We lasted as long as the 20 bucks would go. That was our limit. We didn't ask for refunds or credits. We just weren't ready to bet all we had. Not even if Groucho was doing a bit in the comedy lounge.

Chapter 3: Magical Moments Worth Retelling

Having worked with many companies during my career as a writer, producer, and instructional designer, I have experienced a few of what I call "magical moments." It's where something unexpected occurred or was said that brought a smile to my face or "shook my boat."

I think you know what I mean. A good example was the "Immaculate Reception" by the late Pittsburgh Steeler, Franco Harris. Another, which you can still watch, was a story by the actor Jay Thomas and his experience with the Lone Ranger, Clayton Moore, in Cleveland. Catch it on YouTube. I'll leave the laughing to you.

One such moment occurred when I was working as an instructional designer for a New York production company on a pharmaceutical meeting. The manager of the project, Joanne P., a frustrated writer, told me, "Don't be creative!" That took me by surprise as creativity was the reason most firms hired me.

As a storyteller who has learned to listen-- it's an important tool--many of my friends have related magical moments to me that are worth noting. This chapter contains some of those magical moments worth repeating, along with some of my favorite groaners.

Who Speaks Italian?

A business associate, Richard Feldsman, told me how his father, a lawyer, was in the courtroom one day preparing to handle a case. Another attorney had a witness who only spoke Italian and there was no interpreter in the room. According to his father's testimony, the judge looked down the roll and apparently spotted an attorney named Anthony, with an Italian sounding name like Marzano. He called Anthony up front, and since he was of Italian heritage, the judge wanted him to interpret. Anthony explained that he didn't speak Italian. However, the judge persisted. Anthony then went up to the witness, and moving his hands gesturing up and down as he spoke, which is often stereotyped as an Italian trait, said in English, "What is your name?"

The Christmas Ad

Another classic deals with Christmas. Early in his career as a writer, a longtime friend, Nate Rosenblatt, worked in the promotion department for a company called Rockower Brothers. At the time, Rockower handled the sales of men's and boys' clothing in the Woolco department stores, a modern version of F.W. Woolworth. Nate was charged with putting together the Christmas promotions and artwork for the coming holiday season.

After working diligently on the project for several weeks, Nate proudly brought his effort in to his boss, Don Winokur, on an easel. Don looked at the results for several minutes and said, "Where's Santa Claus? Where are the wreaths, the boxes of presents, the Christmas Trees, and lights? And where is the announcement "Only 20 days to Christmas? This isn't going to work, Nate. There's one thing you'd better remember if you want to work here…You don't f**k with Christmas!"

Adultery

My wife was helping a group of young Catholics prepare for their first holy communion. She overheard a priest listening to a boy's first confession. The boy told the priest he had committed adultery. Startled by the comment, the priest asked, "What do you mean?" The youngster replied, "I was trying to act like an adult."

RFM

My local computer wizard, Alex V., once worked in the IT department of a large company in England. He told me about the time a manager approached him about different computer problems employees were having. Alex showed him his log of complaints and how they were resolved. Looking over the logs, the manager noticed the letters *RFG* on a number of the reported problems. When asked what that meant, Alex replied, "I told them to Read the F**king Manual."

You'll Find It on YouTube

Today, when folks ask me how to resolve a problem with a device, how to replace the batteries in a TV remote, fix a dent in a car, or something similar, I usually have a standard response. I tell them *WFV* (Watch the F**king Video on YouTube." There are always at least one or more videos showing how to accomplish the task successfully.

The Best Date in Years

Another friend, who will remain nameless, operated a small publishing business from his home. Being pretty successful, he was able to hire a representative to promote his products around the country. After three months on the job, the rep, her name was Charlie, came over to provide the boss with a quarterly report on her progress.

Now this friend loved Great Danes and always had one in his office, usually sitting near his desk. After giving her report, Charlie got up to leave. When she did, she accidentally dropped her papers on the floor. As she bent down to pick up the reports, the Great Dane jumped her from behind and wouldn't stop. The boss apologized and tried to pull the dog off, when Charlie said, "Don't worry. That's the best date I've had in years."

Where's the Wound?

My friend, Big Joe, a former EMS provider, says his wife will never let him live down the following experience. Joe and his partner, Steve, received a call about an elderly gentleman who had fallen ill at a Catholic Church during a service on a Wednesday morning in February.

Upon entering the church, Joe saw the man lying in the aisle, and quickly went to work. As he examined the victim, Joe noticed a "T" on the man's forehead. As an EMS he had been taught that a "T" on the forehead meant a tourniquet needed to be applied to the wound. Joe quickly examined the man's arms and legs for the bleed. However, he couldn't find any bleeding. Perplexed, he looked at his partner, Steve, who was standing there laughing. "Joe, look at all the people in the church. They all have the letter "T" on their foreheads. It's Ash Wednesday."

Who was that guy?

My older sister, Betsy, is an interesting character. She has led an exciting life. She was a war correspondent in Vietnam during the 1960's. She went there with her husband, Dirck, a photographer with United Press International. I often said she went there instead of me.

After completing her assignment, which included survival training and flying on B-52 bombing raids, Betsy and her husband returned to the USA. A short time later the couple divorced. She then went to law school in New Orleans, became an EEO lawyer, and worked in the corporate world for several years before starting her own practice in Ohio.

While working as an EEO lawyer for Federated Department Stores, she gave numerous presentations around the country on Equal Employment Opportunity laws. On one trip to deliver a presentation at a hotel in Santa Barbara, CA, Betsy passed a couple as she was parking her car. "Hmm," she said to herself, "That man looks familiar."

Upon entering the hotel and checking in, she passed the same couple again with a similar thought, "I know that man from somewhere." The man briefly glanced at her and kept walking with his partner without saying a word.

On her way home, after the presentation, Betsy thought about her visual encounter in the hotel. Who was that familiar looking man? That night she called her former mother-in-law, Mona, with whom she had maintained a friendship even after the divorce.

Betsy asked, "Was Dirck in Santa Barbara recently?" "Yes, he was." Mona responded. "Funny you should ask. Dirck thought he saw a woman who looked like you at a hotel there but wasn't sure." End of story.

.

Size Matters

My friend, Nathan, and his wife, Margie, always had Great Danes. They recently added a new one to their family. However, the pup's ears were not standing up, which is often a problem with this breed. Their vet suggested they tape empty tampon holders to the dog's ears to keep them up until the muscles in the dog's ears were strong enough to keep them up by themselves. According to the vet the empty containers were about the right size for these animals' ears.

Eager to resolve the problem, the couple stopped at a local CVS on the way home from the veterinarian. Once inside they went directly to the feminine products aisle. There, the couple began examining the wide range of offerings for the product they were searching for. Opening packages one at a time and taking out the tampons to compare their sizes Nathan asked, "Do you think this is the right size?" Margie shook her head. "I think we need to go bigger," she said. "Are you sure?" said Nathan. The conversation and product inspections continued for about 10 minutes before a final decision they could both agree upon was made.

While this discussion was going on, Nathan noticed a young male employee stocking the shelves behind them. From the red, embarrassed look on his face, Nathan could tell he had been listening to part of their conversation. According to Nathan, the young man must have been thinking, "How big a tampon does this lady need?"

The Phone Call

Being able to tell a story, even an untruthful one, can be fun. One day I was on the phone with a friend. He asked me about my family. I began by telling him how my father's family, the Zakroffs, had originally come from Chicago. I then told my friend that the family had a deal with the Capone mob back in the 1930's.

The deal was Al Capone's crew would get the windy city and the Zakroff clan would move to Philadelphia, the city of brotherly love. Suddenly, the line went dead. A few seconds later I called my friend back. "See!" I said, "They're still keeping tabs on us."

The Art of the Deal

Since my father, Louie, ran a small business that required price negotiations on a regular basis, I was familiar with the practice of haggling to get the best deal. It's something I taught my own children at a young age. Two of them are very good at it. The third prefers to buy retail and that's his choice. But it seems not all parents know the "dance" or instill it in their offspring. A friend, Sam Goldman, recently related a tale to me along those lines.

It seems Sam had just asked his girlfriend, Karen, to marry him and wanted to buy her an engagement ring. Not knowing much about diamonds, he asked his future father-in-law, Harry Birnbaum, a clothing wholesaler by trade and known around town for his dealing making prowess, to come with him to Jeweler's Row in Philadelphia, to help him get the best deal on a good stone. He also thought it would be a great way to bond with the man.

Harry, always on the lookout for a great deal, agreed. One Saturday morning the two of them went to one of the many diamond merchants on the Row. Upon entering the building, Harry told Sam to go to another part of the store while he negotiated with the owner for a good deal. While Sam wandered around the store, Harry did his thing. About twenty minutes later, Harry motioned to Sam to come over to the counter.

"What do you think of this deal for that diamond? asked Harry. Sam looked at the stone, smiled, and then replied, "That's super!" Harry looked at his future son-in-law in disgust. "Don't you understand the art here? Get away!" Harry shooed Sam away and then proceeded to close the deal on his own. Sam was perplexed. He had no idea what had just happened, or his role in the process.

Later that day, Harry called his daughter and asked, "Do you really want to marry this schmuck?" Luckily Harry eventually got over the incident. Sam and Karen have been happily married now for over fifty years.

The Test

One film I always enjoy watching is *Diner*. It was produced in 1982 by Barry Levinson. Briefly, here's the story. Billy, played by Timothy Daly returns home to Baltimore to serve as the best man at the upcoming wedding of his childhood buddy Eddie played by Steve Guttenberg.

Billy and Eddie gather with their friends at the local diner, where they exchange stories about their lives. All they really want to do is go back to being the carefree boys they once were, but they know it cannot be. Their funny and at times revealing tales help each other face the mounting responsibility of adulthood.

What caught my attention was the part in the film where Eddie forces his future bride, Elyse, to take and pass a football quiz before the wedding could take place.

When my granddaughter, Natalie, became engaged to her boyfriend, Nick, the idea of giving him some kind of test before the wedding could take place came to my mind. When Nick asked what the test would be on, I told him it would be about our family. I also told him the best way to study for it was to read my first two books.

My younger son, Dennis, was with me at the time. Nick nervously looked at Dennis and asked, "Did you have to take a test?" Dennis smiled and replied, "No! I was born into this family."

Napkins are Napkins.

One of my pickleball friends related a story to me about his childhood. In his youth, Lee spent many summers with his family in Ocean City. One day, when he was eight years old, his family was having friends over for dinner.

As she was preparing the table for a meal with their guests, his mother realized they didn't have any napkins for the table. She asked Lee to run to the store and purchase some.

She gave him a few dollars and off he went. At the store, Lee quickly located a box labeled napkins, paid for them, and then came home. He proudly placed the box on the table. As he did his mother's face turned bright red. Lee had purchased a box of feminine napkins. His mother looked at him. "What?", said the young boy. "Napkins are napkins, right?"

Time Check

Another friend, also named Pete, recently described a cell phone call he witnessed in New Orleans. Pete was in town to close a deal on purchasing a checking cashing business. One of the owners of the business, Ezrah, had just picked him up at the airport and was taking Pete to a hotel. While on the ride, Ezrah's phone rang, He picked it up and was on the call for twenty minutes. After Ezrah hung up, Pete asked him if there was a problem. "Nah," he replied in his New Orleans' drawl. "It was my partner, Keith. If you ask him for the time, he'll tell you how to build a watch."

How Old Are You?

While playing pickleball the other day, I asked a grey-haired fellow how old he was. He replied, "I'm so old I remember when the Dead Sea was just sick."

After getting a great many laughs retelling the answer to my question, I decided to come up with a few of my own. Here they are.

"How old are you?" Answer: "I'm so old I remember when my family was lost in the desert with Moses."

"How old are you?" Answer: "I'm so old I remember when the Grand Canyon was just a creek."

The Senior Tooth Fairy

A friend related the following story to me about his grandmother, Daisey White. Daisey was a very kind and generous lady. She would always go "the extra mile" and do anything to help others. Late in life she suffered from dementia. After living with one of her sons for many years, it became necessary to place her in a nursing home.

A few weeks after her arrival Daisey thought of a great way of endearing herself to her new-found friends at the nursing home. One morning she went to every patient's room, and quietly collected their dentures. She then brought them back to her own room and diligently scrubbed every one of them.

When finished, Daisey placed all the freshly cleaned teeth into a large bowl. It wasn't until later in the day, after receiving calls from residents about missing choppers, that a nurse found the bowl full of dentures in her room. Just imagine the "fun" the nurses had matching the patients to their teeth.

The Great Goof

One of my favorite magazines is The Family Handyman. When I receive a new issue, I immediately flip to the last page and read the two or three stories submitted by homeowners about mistakes they made, from trying to fill a waterbed with a seeping hose, getting stuck on the roof after accidentally kicking away the ladder or to drilling a hole through a pipe behind the wall and causing a leak. As a homeowner for over 50 years, I've had my share of project goofs, so I can relate and chuckle.

Recently, I witnessed a goof that really made me laugh, and because it wasn't one that I made. It was done by a guy who never makes mistakes. You see, I have a neighbor whose name was changed here, not to protect the innocent, as the announcer used to say at the beginning of the old Dragnet TV shows, but in order to retain our friendship.

This neighbor, we'll call him Max, has every tool in the world. He has more tools than a large woodworking shop and completes many challenging tasks that would confuse and confound most homeowners. Max generally plans everything to a T, right down to the number of nails required to complete a project. So, his goof really surprised me.

Max recently added a pool to his property, which increased his need for storing pool toys, umbrellas, and other accessories. To make room for many of his items, he purchased two sheds from a big box store. Why? Because he knew, from being a planner, that one wouldn't hold all of his stuff. Last summer, he built the first shed outside the pool area on a corner of his driveway and filled it. The structure fit perfectly. He could easily open the doors and get things in and out.

This week, Max started assembling the second shed. He had the perfect place for it, near his pool filters between the house and the fence on the other side of his property.

Learning from his experience of building the first shed, he quickly assembled the second one. The last step was to attach the doors. Once he completed that step, he quickly realized his goof. The doors were supposed to swing open, like on the first shed. However, they couldn't because he built the structure too close to the house. The shed fit, but he couldn't open the doors to put anything in it.

I learned of this goof when I saw the disassembled pieces laying up against the fence on his driveway. With my help, Max and I loaded the parts into his pickup truck. He was giving thew shed to his son, Cole, who had recently purchased a house. Hopefully, Cole had enough room to be able to open the doors when it was reassembled.

Footprints in the snow

In Daniel Defoe's famous 1719 novel, Robinson Crusoe leaves the safety of his comfortable middle-class home in England and goes to sea. He is shipwrecked and becomes a castaway and spends 28 years on a remote tropical island near Trinidad. During his time on the island, he meets cannibals, captives, and mutineers. In his 24th year on the island he discovers footprints in the sand. Following those tracks, he ends up meeting a savage from a cannibal tribe whom he named Friday, because that was the day Crusoe found him. Friday provides Crusoe with companionship for several years until he is finally rescued.

When you follow footprints in the sand or the snow, you never know what you may find. A friend, Sally, walks her dog, Jacob, daily in Upper Township just a few miles from the crowded island of Ocean City, NJ. Sally's been known to take her four-legged friend on all manner of hikes around the area. Some of these treks are hours long.

Recently, she saw a post on Facebook about someone in the township thinking they saw a bear in the woods close to her home. In her mind the poster probably mistook what he saw for the Newfoundland dog owned by a friend in town, as these dogs by their large size and dark coats could easily be mistaken for bears.

Several days later, after a snowstorm, Sally took her pup out for their daily constitutional into the woods near her home. As they traveled deeper into the pine forest, she noticed a large set of footprints in the snow in front of them. At first, she thought nothing of it. The tracks might be from the neighbor's Newfoundland. These dogs would leave large paw prints as they played in the snow. Then it hit her, that pet had recently passed. So, it couldn't be him.

Sally then made another discovery. This one spooked her. There were no human footprints accompanying the large paw prints in the snow. A closer examination of the tracks in the snow was puzzling. These weren't like any dog paw prints she had seen. The front feet appeared blocky, with a somewhat rectangular pad. The small, rounded heel pad appeared in the tracks as a circle separate from and below the foot pad. And there were claws. The claw prints on the front feet were longer and showed up farther from the toes in the tracks. Was there a big foot or a bear in the woods?

Sally didn't wait to find out. Before you could say Robinson Crusoe, she and her little companion made a quick exit from the woods. If she ever saw large paw prints unaccompanied by human footprints on her walks she and Jacob would immediately retreat to the safety of her home. She was certain this didn't happen on a Friday.

Immigrants from Avalon

With all the talk about immigration in this country and problems at the border, I recently learned about a local incident that occurred in Cape May County around 2009 and still stinks to this very day.

Here's the lowdown. It seems the island borough of Avalon, the one with all the McMansions, had a problem with a certain group of inhabitants. Their family name was Mephitidae. Sounds Greek to me, but let's not be prejudiced by ethnicities. From the reports I read there were about 74 of them, including grandparents, spouses, and children.

It appears that the town was not happy with this family and forcibly expelled them from the locale. Yes, in America! Not only did they remove the family, but they forcibly put a number of them in cages and dropped them off at different locations throughout the county without informing any of those nearby towns of who was coming and when. I guess because of the short distance they didn't use buses like the governors of Florida and Texas to transport them. They also separated families without any care or concern for the possible ramifications. And, there were no plans to reunite the family at a future date.

In addition, due to the lack of notifications, there was no welcoming committee to meet these immigrants from Avalon, nor was there a means for providing them with food and adequate shelter. As a result, many of the new arrivals, though friendly, went door to door looking for handouts.

These actions lead to a great number of complaints by residents in Upper Township, just south of Ocean City. The mayor of the town told reporters that he recognized Avalon's need to solve its own issues but didn't want his town to pay the price. Just think of the need for the additional resources required based on the unplanned increase in the local population. Education and recreation are just a few examples.

Why remind people of this problem now? Because. On a recent trip through Upper Township, I passed by a member of the Mephitidae family. Sadly, his remains were scattered across the road. Apparently, he didn't cross the highway in a designated area. Maybe because he never had the opportunity to learn how to read.

I could tell he was a member of that family by the white stripe on his back and the smell that hit me a few seconds later.

The Odyssey of Hefe Le Pew

A friend told me about this incident. It's a follow up on the previous story. Here's my creative/fun take on it.

Hefe le Pew was a royal member of the Mephitidae family. He was born in Avalon, a town of large villas and castles by the ocean. However, at a young age he and his clan were exiled from the city. The family was torn apart by the city's rulers and shipped off to different parts of the world with little hope of ever uniting. Before the banishment, his parents had imparted to him knowledge of the family's great and storied history including great uncle Pepe, who spent many years searching for the one true love of his life, Penelope.

Inspired by the tales of his adventurous uncle, Hefe set out on a journey to find his own Penelope. For years he roamed his known world, which included South Jersey, in search of his one true love. However, Hefe had one problem. He was near-sighted. On many a sojourn he mistook someone else for his treasured lover.

One such occasion occurred in Upper Township. On a bright sunny day, after weeks into his search, Hefe thought he had finally found his Penelope. From a distance he spied a large dark animal that he imagined could be his consort forever. "This had to be Penelope," he thought.

Hefe, with blind love in his heart, quickly approached the animal. "This had to be her," he kept saying to himself. As he grew closer, he could tell his perceived consort had noticed him. When he finally got within three feet of his dream, he could finally see that it wasn't Penelope. His eyes and his heart had betrayed him. Standing in front of Hefe was Jake, a large Rottweiler mix, ready to defend his master's castle. Realizing he was in deep trouble, Hefe turned to run. As he did, Jake grabbed him by his tail.

Hearing the commotion, Sally and her husband, Keith, Jake's owners, ran outside. What they saw was Jake holding Hefe's tail in his mouth and twirling him around and around over his head. Hefe quickly sensed there was no love for him here. Frightened and using his best defensive mechanism, Hefe not only sprayed Jake with the family perfume, but also the entire the yard, as well as Sally and Keith.

A few seconds later Jake finally released Hefe's tail. At that moment Hefe scooted into the woods. In the aftermath, Jake, Sally, and Keith were, to put it lightly, a smelly mess. It took Sally, Keith, and Jake several hours and gallons of tomato juice to rid themselves of Hefe's potion. In the meantime, Hefe, never wanting to make such a mistake again, made an appointment with a local optometrist hoping to get a pair of contacts before he continued his search for Penelope.

A Case of Mistaken Identity

When you tell someone a tale about a skunk, like the previous story, more often than not, they have one of their own to relate. Here's one for you.

My friends, Chris and Pam, live in Churchville, PA, a rustic suburban community outside of Philadelphia. They love the area because it feels like the country. When they go on trips or vacations, their neighbors, Rob and Sue Thomas, feed their cat, Abbey. Pam and Chris reciprocate for Willie, a wily black and white cat who rules the roost at the Thomas household. It was a convenient arrangement for both families.

On one occasion, while Rob and Sue were vacationing, Chris, responsible for feeding Willie, was working late on a business project. About 11 pm he remembered that he hadn't fed Willie and ran next door to complete his task.

Once inside, Chris opened a can of cat food and placed it in Willie's dish. Since Willie liked to stay outside, Chris opened the back door and called him, "Here Willie. Here's your dinner." There was no moon that night and no lights at the rear of the house. Out of the darkness, a very different black and white figure approached the door.

Out of the corner of his eye Chris saw it, but it was too late. "You're not Willie!" he yelled. Before Chris could move, the startled critter raised its tail and gave Chris a large dose of its scented liquid. Not exactly Chanel No. 5.

Covered with the spray and stinking to high heaven, Chris ran home and banged on the back door of his home for help. Pam, unaware of what had just happened, was awakened by the noise, and thought about calling the police. It was then she realized that Chris wasn't in the house.

Pam turned on the outside lights. She could see Chris through the kitchen window. She could also smell him through the glass. Quickly assessing the situation, she grabbed a can of tomato juice, opened it, and tossed the can to Chris along with a towel. "Take a shower outside with the hose and the juice before you dare come in here," shouted Pam.

From that day on, Chris promised never again to wait until dark to feed Willie, no matter how busy he was. But just in case, Pam made sure there was always a bright, charged flashlight near the back door, as well as an ample supply of tomato juice and a towel. She also printed out silhouette pictures of a cat and a skunk and hung them on the refrigerator so Chris could distinguish between the two animals when he went to feed Willie.

The Battery

I have a ten-year-old Timex Expedition watch that I wear to the beach. The battery usually lasts a year or two. In the past, when I needed a new battery, I would go to a local jewelry store in Egg Harbor Township. However, that store closed. I then looked online for another jewelry store that replaced watch batteries. I found one in Northfield, NJ, which was about 8 miles from my home. After checking their hours of operation, I went there on a Monday morning. It took less than 12 minutes to replace the battery, and I was on my way.

A few days later, I received a cellphone call from my neighbor, Steve. He was out shopping with his wife and wanted to know where he could get a new battery for his Casio watch. I immediately told him where to go as he was close to the jewelry store in Northfield.

Long story short, he didn't get there on that particular day. A week later, I asked him if he had gotten the battery for his Casio. "Funny you should ask," he said. "I went there and gave the owner my watch to replace the battery. He came back a short time later and told me he couldn't change the battery. When I asked why, I learned the watch doesn't have a battery. It's solar powered!"

Favorite Groaners

For some reason, I can remember a wide range of jokes and punchlines. Maybe I'm just looking to laugh more. Every once in a while, someone will say something during a conversation about who knows what and one of these "laughers" pops into my mind and given a chance, I'll tell it. Here are a few to groan over.

Equal Employment Opportunity

The CEO of a large company needed a secretary. He spread ads all over town. A few days later, there was a knock on his door. It was a dog. He had a newspaper in his mouth. He came in, put the newspaper on a desk, opened it to the classifieds page and pointed to the ad that the CEO had placed.

The CEO was impressed. But he thought it was a joke, so he playfully decided to test the dog. "I need a secretary who understands the basics of computers," he said.

The dog went to one of the secretaries' desks, climbed onto the chair, turned on the router and the computer, in total tranquility. The CEO was amazed, but decided to go further:

"I need a secretary who understands spreadsheets."

The dog quickly opened Excel, grabbed a stack of papers, and started scanning names and contacts. The astonished CEO desperately followed:

"I need a bilingual secretary!"

The dog turned to the CEO and replied, "Meow."

The Three Surgeons

After finishing a round of golf on a Wednesday afternoon, three surgeons were in the locker room of their country club considering the work they were scheduled to perform the next day.

Before long, the discussion drifted to who were the easiest people to perform surgery on. One surgeon said it was accountants. "You cut them open, and everything adds up."

The second surgeon disagreed. "It's engineers," he said. "When you open them up there's a schematic inside telling you where everything is."

Looking at the pair, the third chuckled and spoke up. "You're both wrong! It's lawyers. You open them up. You'll find there's no heart and no guts, plus the mouth and rear end are interchangeable."

The Talking Dog Story

An outdoorsman was riding through the mountains of Colorado when he noticed a sign by the roadside. The sign read, "Talking Dog for Sale." Intrigued, he followed the signs to a cabin a few miles up the trail. He parked his jeep and walked up to the cabin. There he saw a man sitting on the porch. He asked the man, "Is this the place with the talking dog for sale?" "Yes," replied the man. "He's around back if you want to see him."

The curious outdoorsman walked to the back yard and gazed upon a large German Shepard lying there with several pups around it.

"Are you the talking dog?" asked the outdoorsman. "Yes, I am." replied the Shepard. After getting over the amazement of the reply, the man asked, "What's your story."

Over the next few minutes, the dog related how as a young pup he could understand English and had the gift of speech. With these skills he worked for the CIA gathering intel from unsuspecting spies. Then, for several years he worked at large airports with the TSA sniffing out drugs, but recently decided to retire and raise a family.

"Amazing," said the man.

After finishing his discussion with the German Shepard, the outdoorsman walked back around to the front of the cabin and asked the man sitting there how much he wanted for the dog.

"Ten dollars," replied the man. "Ten dollars for a talking dog!"

"Yep," said the man. "He's a liar. He never did any of that stuff."

Only in Brooklyn
A rabbi walks into a bar with a parrot on his shoulder. The bartender looks at the pair and asks, "Where did you get him?" The parrot replies, "Brooklyn, we've got thousands of them there."

The Condor and the Toad

A toad is hopping around the desert floor in search of food when a large condor sweeps down from above and swallows the creature in one gulp. The toad passes through the bird's digestive system and looks out and down at the ground from the condor's rear end and yells, "How high are we?" The condor replies, "About 300 feet." To that the toad then said, "You wouldn't sh*t me, would you?"

The Untold Story of Washington Crossing the Delaware

People often wonder where expressions come from. Some are based on historic facts like "It's raining cats and dogs" or "The pot calling the kettle black." Here's the untold story behind another famous expression which dates back to the American Revolution.

It was Christmas eve in the year 1776. George Washington and his troops had left Valley Forge and were crossing the Delaware river at night on the way to attack the Hessian soldiers holding Trenton, New Jersey.

At the front of Washington's boat was Corporal Tom Peters. Peters was standing up holding a lantern pointing the way across the river. Washington's boat was suddenly hit by a wave and Corporal Peters went tumbling overboard. After unsuccessfully searching for the corporal, Washington continued his journey across the river to the Jersey side.

Wet, tired, and sad, Washington and his troops continued their mission south towards Trenton. Just outside the city, Washington spotted a house with a light on. He went and knocked on the door. To his surprise a madam answered the door. It was a house of ill repute. Freezing in the winter's night air, the general asked for aid and comfort. The madam agreed and asked, "How many are you?" Washington turned around and counted. He then replied, "Twenty-nine, without Peters." To which the madam said, "You got to be sh*ting me!"

Entomology Profiling

It's late spring and a bumble bee was on the prowl for pollen to bring back to the hive. During his trek he crosses paths with another bee. This one is loaded with the sweet rewards from a successful hunt.

"Where'd you get all that stuff?" asked the insect on the prowl.

"The Goodman Bar Mitzvah over in the next yard," replied the other bee.

"But what's that on your head?" the bumble bee asked."

"Oh, that's a yarmulke (pronounced ya-ma-kah). I'd didn't want to be mistaken for a wasp."

The Classical Music Lover

Joshua Michaels taught classical music at the Juilliard School of Music for many years. He especially loved the work of Ludwig Von Beethoven. When finally given an opportunity to travel to Vienna, he immediately went to the grave of his idol.

Standing at the grave site he heard music emanating from the ground below. As a lover of the great composer's music, he recognized it as the Ninth Symphony, but being played in reverse. Startled, he called the Vienna Music Society on his cell phone and asked if someone could come to the cemetery. Within 30 minutes, Johann Schmitt, the director of the prestigious organization arrived. By this time, the music resembled Beethoven's Fourth Symphony, again being played in reverse.

Amazed, both onlookers called over to the groundskeeper and asked if he had heard this before. The worker replied, "Yah! He's just decomposing."

Chapter 4: The Ocean City Chronicles

Ocean City's tourist slogan reads "America's Greatest Family Resort." I have been known to agree with it, but only for 9 months of the year: from September through May. Then forget it. The following stories encompass many of my thoughts about this seashore town that has been our home for more than 20 years.

Jurassic Island

There have been countless films titled Jurassic this and Jurassic that with plots about carnivorous and herbivorous creatures interacting with homo sapiens and the tragic results. These films focus on a remote island off the coast of Costa Rica. However, for more than 20 years we've been living on a Jurassic Island of sorts only 65 miles from Philadelphia, PA, often with similar results.

Though we are surrounded by water, we share this island with voracious cervidae who cross over from the mainland at low tide. Vulpes vulpes of the order carnivora often roam the streets in search of prey, unafraid of humans. Hundreds of oryctolagus cuniculus crisscross the island feasting on flowers and bushes of every variety, and they reproduce like crazy. No need for cloning. As Ian Malcolm, played by Jeff Goldblum in *Jurassic Park*, said, "In nature, life will find a way." Fresh litters appear every four to six weeks.

Our island is also home to a countless number of Sciuridae which have an average lifespan of 2 to 8 years. They scale trees and fences with ease, chew cable wires and relish the rubber coating inside cars' engine compartments. Should you be foolish enough to attempt to trap one of these critters, they will instantly go into a rage, sneer, and threaten to bite your hand off.

Thankfully, one group of predators we no longer have to fear on the island is pterodactyls. They died out thousands of years ago. However, they have been replaced by flocks of branta bernicla. These feathery, winged critters leave their droppings on the athletic fields and also indiscriminately target people and cars. It pays to keep your eyes on the skies as well as where you are stepping.

Occasionally, a furry, flat-tailed castor will emerge from the bay and check out the lumber supply to construct a prehistoric McMansion. Many an inhabitant has been tricked by a ferocious looking *didelphis virginiana* feasting on the delicacies left by tourists in an open trash can, or just playing possum. Wide cracks or visible holes in an attic or roof will immediately attract families of procyon labor and they are tough to get rid of.

In the winter, as the temperature drops, many garages become home to pairs of apodemus sylvaticus. If left unchecked, they will turn the space into a playground for their offspring. If you happen to live near the water or on a lagoon you can expect a visit from the fearful looking ondatra zibethicus. They have been around for thousands of years and consider you to be the intruder. To some folks these critters appear to be rattus (rats), but they are not. Rats can't afford the real estate taxes.

Translations:

Cervidae: deer. order Artiodactyla, Vulpes vulpes: red fox, Apodemus sylvaticus: field mouse, Oryctolagus cuniculus: rabbit, Sciuridae: squirrel, branta bernicla: type of Canadian geese, Castor: beaver, Procyon lotor: raccoon, Ondatra zibethicus: muskrat, Rattus: rat.

Paradise Lost

In high school or college, many of us were introduced to or forced to read *Paradise Lost,* an epic poem by the 17th-century English poet John Milton. It's a telling of the biblical tale of the Fall of Mankind – the moment when Adam and Eve were tempted by Satan to eat the forbidden fruit from the Tree of Knowledge. God then banished them from the Garden of Eden forever.

How does that relate to Ocean City? What was once a summer paradise is now one screen door from hell. Numerous longtime residents have left of their own accord, "banished" by increased real estate taxes, over the top property values, or just being tired of overcrowding.

OC's total number of year-round residents ranges between 10,000 and 12,000, depending upon whom you ask. From Memorial Day to Labor Day the number of daily inhabitants swells to well over 150,000, not including dogs and an ever-growing population of rabbits.

In the more than fifty years since we started coming to Ocean City, it has changed drastically. In the 1970's it was still a quiet Methodist-founded town with street after street of bungalows, duplexes, and single-family homes. Summer residents rented the same properties for a week, two weeks, a month, and if they could afford it, for the summer, year after year. Rents were affordable.

What was once a paradise is now a crowded metropolis of concrete and macadam. Where once a single family-friendly bungalow stood, it has been demolished and replaced by two McMansions. Almost every inch of ground is now covered with concrete or pavers. Rainwater has no place to go. A number of homes being constructed don't fit the look and feel of the neighborhood they're being built in. Many new homes have small pools that you can't really swim in. I refer to them as toilets. They're mostly status symbols used by folks too lazy to go to the beach or who possibly can't swim.

When you replace a bungalow with two large homes, where there may have been two cars, they have multiplied like rabbits into four or more. Parking has become a problem. Besides the increase in cars, the new mode of transportation is the electric golf cart, which may seat anywhere from two to eight people, usually with young kids at the rear, holding on for dear life. Though they only have a maximum speed of about 25 mph, some of these open vehicles whip up and down streets with little care for their passengers or oncoming traffic. Stopping at stop signs has become optional.

Everyone seems to be in a hurry. Folks on bikes do not know about or refuse to follow the rules. In OC they are considered motor vehicles. Many bike riders are on their cellphones. Others have earbuds and are oblivious to motor vehicles approaching behind them. No one wants to take responsibility. It is always the other person's fault.

If visitors decide to hit the beach, a lot are uneducated about beach etiquette. They place their towels and chairs right next to yours, less than 10 feet away. They play loud music and leave it blasting even when they are not there. They feed the seagulls – a real "No-No" - and against the law, or they leave food uncovered, which more often than not can easily be spotted and dive-bombed by these keen-eyed scavengers.

Latecomers to the beach set up their chairs right in front of your ocean view, not caring or knowing that within the next hour or so, the tide will be coming in. When it does, they simply move right on top of you. Some privileged sun worshipers don't buy beach tags. When they see the taggers coming, they simply walk off the beach or run and hide in the water until the taggers move on.

Ocean City is known for its great boardwalk. However, one must be careful of the time they choose to visit. Before noon from Memorial Day to Labor Day is not the best. That is when, without having to purchase a ticket, you think you're watching the Tour de France live, as the bike enthusiasts roar up and down the boards at break-neck speeds.

OC goes out of its way for bike-riders. There are set lanes on various streets. However, this is often an inconvenience, so they take to the alleys. More times than not a family of bikers starting from 3 or 4 years of age with training wheels up to fifty plus will suddenly appear in front of you. Why? because they are on vacation and not responsible for looking both ways when they come to a street, according to them.

Another place that used to be part of this paradise is the Aquatic and Fitness Center. For some reason, this jewel of the city has been allowed to fall into a state of disrepair, especially the pool. It is often cold and not as clean as it used to be. In addition, the power chair enabling folks with disabilities to enter and exit the water is often out of service and in need of repair. Some residents now call the center in advance to find out the water temperature. If it is cold, they won't come. I have been led to believe that the city is purchasing the pool heater parts from North Korea. The parts come with a five-day warranty and after exactly five days they break.

The use of modern technology has also helped to destroy this island paradise. Where once you simply went to a local bakery to purchase sweet treats with an idea of what you wanted in advance, you now stand in long lines as millennials, with phones in hand, show their spouses pictures of the treats in the case, while twenty other people in line breathlessly await her decision.

Remember, Methodists founded this paradise, and there are many churches in town of different denominations. Looking at the full parking lots on Sundays, you would think the buildings were full of worshippers. But it's not religious folks, its sun worshippers filling up the spaces and spending the day on the beach.

Ah, if only we could return the town to the paradise it once was. Give Satan back his apple. But let's face it, the garden is lost and gone forever.

Nightmare in Menace

Usually around Halloween, there's a swarm of horror films on TV and shown in movie theaters across the country.

These classics always include every version of *"A Nightmare on Elm Street"* and *"Friday the 13th"*. They all star Freddy Krueger as the villainous slasher haunting the neighborhood. Spruce Road also has it villains but it's never on a Friday or the 13th.

Once a year the folks in Ocean City hold a boat parade on a Saturday evening around the third weekend in July. The exact date depends upon the tides. Sometimes the boats in the affair number around a hundred or so. It depends upon the economy and the price of fuel. Those who do not own boats but live on the bay or lagoons decorate their houses and compete for prizes. The town calls the event "Night in Venice." I call it "Nightmare in Menace."

That night is also a great excuse for summer parties, some very extravagant. Though Ocean City is a "dry" town on this night you would not know it. All day long ice trucks roll up and down the streets delivering ice in preparation for the night's parties. Trucks loaded with rented tents, tables and chairs also deliver their contents to planned parties all over the island.

Many streets near the bay or the lagoons are blocked off with barricades. Parking is prohibited on certain streets. To ease traffic the town offers a jitney service to take attendees to places where they can watch the boat parade. At around 4:00 pm the crowds begin to converge on the parade locations and parties. Invitees of all ages walk up our street carrying boxes of food, cakes, cases of beer, and containers full of spirits and who knows what. Sounds like great fun. It is. Living across from a lagoon or surrounded by parties, we accept the noise from the bands and DJs as it is only one night. And most music stops at midnight.

However, there are always a few villains who spoil the night for us and our neighbors through acts of mischief or drunken stupidity. If invited to a party, we leave early. If we are staying home, we turn on all the outside lights and sit outside on the porch to dissuade any troublemakers.

Since there are never enough parking spots for party goers, many park illegally hoping not to get hit, cause an accident, or get a ticket. After the parties have closed down, some of these rogues are so drunk they cannot find their way home and sleep on the sidewalk. My granddaughter, out for a morning run the next day, found one lying next to the curb. She didn't know if he was a possible victim of Freddy or alive. He finally let out a grunt, which indicated he was the latter rather than the former.

We've also had gross experiences. On another morning after one of these affairs, we thought, by the odor, a dog had left his business behind one of our cars. On closer examination and uncovering the source of the smell, we discovered handprints on the trunk of one of our cars. We could tell they weren't Freddy's. However, the stinker left a deposit just below it that you couldn't take to the bank.

How about a discount for your first sale of the day?

Ocean City loves events. They keep the local economy going. Traditional offerings include shows at the music pier, the Doh Dah parade, Night in Venice, boardwalk races, and sand sculpturing contests. However, two of the city's biggest events are the spring and fall block parties.

These attractions, weather permitting, attract thousands of people. During the first weekend in May and on Columbus (Indigenous peoples) weekend, Ocean City holds their block parties on Asbury Avenue. The events stretch from 5th street up to 14th street. On this more than a mile long affair there are tents and booths of vendors set up on both sides of the avenue.

The vendors' offerings include seasonal wreathes of every color and size, fresh pickles, Greek baked goods, doggie treats, the work of artists and photographers, wood carvings, women's and baby clothing, T-shirts and sweatshirts, coffee, food, and local charities. You will also find realtors, carpet companies, bakeries, fishing gear, antiques, fresh and dried flowers, soda, restaurants, pretzels, and of course Johnson's Carmel Corn, as well as unsold clothing from the previous season.

When we attend, my wife and I go early. We park about two blocks away on Simpson and walk up to 14th street. However, crossing West at 14th street is always a challenge. Although there's a traffic light and you can push a button to indicate you want to cross, you can take your life in your hands. The light never stays green long enough to safely cross. There should be audible advisories at the light telling you to get your tail in gear and run to the opposite curb.

Although the start time is listed as 9:00, when we arrive just before then there is usually a small crowd already on the street examining the offerings. It seems a flower vendor always has the same spot on the corner of 14th and Asbury. One year, right next to them was a booth featuring an array of home-made crafts and antiques. As we walked by a snowman lantern caught our eye. We thought it would look great on our front porch at Christmas. Jokingly, I said to the lady manning the booth, "How about a discount for your first sale of the day?" Unexpectedly, she said, "Okay!" and took five dollars off the price. You never know unless you ask.

Having attended both block parties for more than 20 years, we look for certain vendors or something different that catches our attention. If we do buy something, something at home has to go to make room for it. Storage space is always at a premium with a shore home.

One thing we never get used to is the need for people to bring their dogs to these events. They attend in all shapes and sizes. Baby carriages are also a problem with the crowded street. When the two collide, it can be a catastrophe. Take for instance the time we witnessed a parent purchase a pretzel stick for their little boy sitting in a coach. He had just proudly placed the stick in his mouth. As they passed through the crowd a large dog took it right out of his mouth. The little boy cried, and the dog had a morning snack.

Our treks through the block parties usually last just over an hour up and back, as we make our way from 14th street down to 6th. We seldom go past 6th street as the booths on the street below it are normally of little interest to us.

By the time we begin our return trip, the crowds have swelled making the walk back almost impossible. When this occurs, we usually take to the sidewalks to make it safely back to 14th street and then take our lives in our hands once more as we put our butts in gear and race across West Avenue back to our car.

Door Dash Dummies

When one hears the name Door Dash, most folks think of a food delivery company. You know, the one that will pick up your order from a restaurant and bring it to your front door for a small charge and possibly a tip. That is, if the order is delivered quickly and is still warm.

In the Riviera section of Ocean City, many residents think about door dash differently. In this neighborhood we have an infestation of little demons. It is often said that intelligence skips a generation, sometimes two. There's often proof of it on a warm night and even sometimes during the day.

Our island offers a wide range of activities for children including all types of organized sports, acting and art classes, surfing, and more. Just check out the town's website. However, there is a group of delinquents too dumb to take advantage of them, as well as parents who apparently don't know or care where their offspring are or what they are doing.

Consider this. You're sitting in your living room on a summer eve, relaxing and watching a TV show or chatting with some friends. Suddenly there's a loud bang or two on the front door that makes the house shake. What do you do? If you're like most folks, you get up and run to the door. When you open it, there's no one there. The door dash demons have struck again. In the distance you can hear laughter and catch a glimpse of several young boys running down the street away from your home.

If you are a senior, and possibly have an illness or heart condition, the so-called "harmless prank" can immediately bring on anger, a feeling of rage, and possibly trigger a 911 call. Chasing after the demons is useless. Calling the police results in a patrol car driving through the neighborhood, but the culprits have long gone by the time officers arrive.

My family, as well as several others have been victims of these demon attacks multiple times. On one occasion, after an attack, I actually waited a while, exited my home by a side door and quietly walked down the street. The group, having thought they made a clean getaway, were returning to the scene of their crime, possibly to hit another home. When they saw me, they ran.

I cornered two of them in the bushes a few houses away. I was smart enough to not touch them as they mouthed off and ran past me into the darkness. However, I was able to give the police a description of the two jerks I had boxed in. I even recognized one of them as a bully from one street over who was always causing trouble.

The next day, one of my neighbors received an apology from a parent whose son had told his parents what he had done. The parent thought it was this particular neighbor's house that had been targeted.

Now that you understand the problem, let me tell you about how brilliant these geniuses are. My wife likes to read. On a warm sunny day, when it is not too windy, you'll find her curled up with a good book or her iPad and sitting on the front porch. A few days after the last incident, while engrossed in her tome, two of these bright pranksters came up the front steps on to the porch, not seeing my wife, they began banging on the front door.

"What are you doing?" she yelled. Completely startled and ready to wet their pants they ran away. Hearing the commotion, I came out. Terry told me what happened. By this time the two culprits had thought about what they had done and were coming back up the street to apologize.

I walked down the street to meet them. I asked why they had hit our house again and again. Their excuse was that they had been told to do it by the neighborhood bully. They were also told there was no harm in it. Plus, it was great fun. I explained the harm, got their names, and addresses. I let them go this time but warned of the consequences if it ever happened again. So far, so good.

How Difficult an Order?

As a kid, growing up in the 1950's, I fondly remember one of the characters in Popeye cartoons, Wimpy. He would always say, I'd gladly pay you Tuesday for a hamburger today." As a burger lover, I often order the sandwich for lunch in my quest for the ultimate burger.

On one particular Tuesday during a recent summer in Ocean City, I ordered one from a restaurant we hadn't visited before. Tell me, "How tough is it to get a burger the way you like it?" Being a burger connoisseur, I like my burgers plain, but pink in the middle. I don't eat cheese. I tell the wait staff, if they don't know me or if it's my first visit to the establishment, to keep the lettuce, tomato, and onion. I jokingly also say "Give me a discount because you don't have to put that stuff on my sandwich. Just give me the burger medium on a fresh bun and hot French fries. "

Often, when they bring my burger to the table, I'll cut it in half, just to make sure its pink in the middle, not bloody. If it's not that way, I'll often send it back to the kitchen and ask for another. That's just me. I'm paying for it and that's how I like it.

When at a restaurant, I always let my wife order first. I was always taught to let the woman go first. When it's my turn to order I'll often say to the waitress, "This is going to be difficult, but hopefully you can get my order right." After I give them my order they'll often say, "That's not difficult. That should be easy. We can do that!"

More often than not they cannot. On this particular Tuesday we tried a restaurant at a local hotel. I ordered a burger. I told the server, Wendy, how I wanted it; medium. "Just the burger and the bun with fries," I said. After an extremely long wait at an almost empty establishment just after noon, the meal arrived. It was a cheeseburger. Not what I ordered! Wendy apologized and took it back to the kitchen.

About ten minutes later she reappeared with another burger. This one wasn't coated with cheese, but it wasn't medium either which I could tell by cutting it in half. It was well done. Not a speck of pink. Apparently, according to our server, they had switched it with another customer's order, someone a few tables over whom I had heard request a well-done cheeseburger. They must have kept it warm for him under a heat lamp.

Though my wife's meal, a quiche, was fine, mine wasn't. If they couldn't get a difficult order like a plain burger right, why go back? I certainly will not.

Popcorn John and the Amazing Basil Plants

In the spring of 2022, I put four basil plants in my small, raised garden bed in the back of yard of our home. Each grew to more than three feet in height. Having more of this herb than we could use, we offered fresh basil leaves to our neighbors and friends. My next-door neighbor, Steve, came for his portion and cut his own. Neighbor Matt, from down the block, gladly took some cuttings for his wife's cooking. My wife also took some cuttings for her pool friends, Bonnie and Kathy.

Then, one warm Saturday night, about dusk, as we were sitting on the front porch on a beautiful late July evening, a lady on a bike pulled up in front of the house and asked, "Is this the Zakroffs'?" A little surprised, I answered, "Yes! Can I help you?' She responded by saying, "I'm John Stauffer's wife. I understand you have basil." "Oh! You're Popcorn John's wife." I said. She smiled and replied "Yes."

A few seconds later John Stauffer himself appeared on his bike. John is the owner of Ocean City's famous Johnson's Popcorn. My sons, Steve and Dennis, had worked for him years ago. I often see John in the pool at the Ocean City Aquatic and Fitness Center.

I asked John and his wife to move their bikes off the street. It wasn't safe to ride bikes let alone park them on the street when it's getting dark, especially on a summer night. They brought their bikes to the sidewalk, and I agreed to cut a bunch of fresh basil for them from our crop.

As I went into the house to get a pair of scissors and a bag for the herbs, I passed one of my sons, Steve, working at the dining room table. I told him who was outside. Steve went out front to chat with John, as I made my way to the garden to complete the Stauffer's "order."

As they left with their supply of basil, I just shook my head in disbelief. "Who comes out on a busy Saturday night in the summer for basil?" They must really be amazing plants. I guess I should have just put out a sign advertising Amazing Basil for Friends.

The plants kept supplying us with fresh basil until the first frost, when Mother Nature finally said, "Enough!"

The Basil Bandit

This is a follow-up to the previous tale. A year later, seeing John in the pool at the Aquatic and Fitness Center, I mentioned to him that we again had fresh basil and to let us know if he wanted some. John said he would check with his wife and trade us a container of Johnson's Popcorn for the herb.

Two days later, this time on a weekday afternoon, John appeared at our door with a large container of popcorn and a request. His wife wanted basil, but she wanted to cut her own. I said, "Okay!" How much basil could she take?

The next afternoon, while we were out, John's wife came to our garden and cut several bunches. We were a little surprised at the quantity she took. However, being amazing plants, we knew the crop would eventually grow back.

Several weeks later we were returning from an off-island shopping. While coming up the alley behind our house, we saw a lady loading two large bunches of basil into the basket on her bike and riding past us. My wife, Terry, and I just looked at each other in surprise. What was going on here? A quick survey of the garden revealed missing basil. Had we been hit by a basil bandit?

Later that evening, my grandson, Stephen, noticed a large container of Johnson's Popcorn at our back door. Apparently, the culprit was John Stauffer's wife. She had left her family's signature "calling card" in trade for some of our amazing basil.

Mister Exit 63 and the Prime Rib Dinner

For a number of years before COVID-19, a friend from the pool, Jim O'Donnell, a chef by trade and culinary instructor at Ocean County Vo-Tech, invited a few of us up to his school for a prime rib dinner before Christmas break. Chef Jim told Ted, one of our group of water rats at the pool, to pass the word around about the meal and to provide directions to the school in Ware Township, New Jersey, just off the Garden State Parkway.

Getting up there in age (the exact number is a secret) and not having driven there himself, Ted spread the word. However, he got the exit number on the Parkway wrong. He told potential diners it was Exit 63. How many diners would get off at Exit 63 and be looking for Ted and the school?

Luckily, the folks checked with a few other invitees as to the correct exit. Otherwise, they'd still be looking for the school or be lost in the Wharton State Forest forever and eventually devoured by the Jersey Devil.

As usual, the meal was great for those who found the school. Chef Jim also provided us with some goodies to take home for our families to enjoy. However, for many days after the event, Ted became known as Mister Exit 63, but that wasn't even close to his age.

Sneaky Pete and the Regulars

I've been playing pickleball for about 10 years, long before the sport became so popular. It now shows up in some form on many television commercials and in professional tournaments broadcast on ESPN.

On most Tuesday and Thursday mornings, year-round, along with myself, the pickleball regulars show up to play at the Upper Township Community Center on Route 50. The building, which was once a candle factory, comes to life around 8:35 am. That's when the regulars start arriving in the parking lot one car or truck at a time, followed by two or three more. The players patiently wait in their vehicles until about 8:45 when we are given a signal by Barbara, the building custodian, to enter.

The players then muster their way into the building, passing by the office of Larry Cole, who oversees the sports programs at the building. Most players give him a smile and a warm hello.

Like a bunch of elves knowing their tasks, the early regulars sign in. Then they move the protective pads and trash cans into position to prevent balls from going behind the bleachers. They also raise the basketball nets and set up several pickleball nets – there's room for four - and bring out a bag of balls.

The balls, plus a first aid kit and ice packs are supplied through donations from the players. When you pickle at Upper you play for fun and are required to have a smile on your face. Those are the rules!

The oldest of the regulars is Bob Swartz, a former truck driver, who lives nearby in a retirement community. Bob loves to argue about whether a ball is in or out. I relish challenging Bob on his calls. I often tell him we'll check the video with New York for a fair opinion.

There's also Ward Reese, a tall, lanky player in his late seventies who knows how to put a spin on the ball. Ward has more fused bones than a plumbing system but manages to get out on the court and make a strong accounting of himself.

On many a Tuesday morning, you'll find Maggie Lundgate sitting in her bronze-colored Subaru waiting for the "okay" to come in the building. Maggie loves to play and has had a few injuries as a result of her desire to win. If she's not there it's because one of her grandkids is under the weather or she's pulled a muscle from overdoing it.

From April through January, you'll find partners Joanne and Chris from Somers Point being counted as regulars. They're usually the first folks in the parking lot on Tuesdays and Thursdays. They've got the setup routine down to a science and know where all the pieces fit. Joanne's game has greatly improved since she started, and Chris, her partner, is a natural.

Another regular is Ray Matricardi. He was involved in construction before retiring. Ray is a good player with a great sense of humor. He's always smiling and never gets down no matter what the score.

I also count as regulars those players who show up several times a month. This group includes Jackie Z., a trim lady from Northfield, Mary Beth, a retired middle school math teacher from Upper Township, and Steve Rothfarb, a former radiologist from Millville (There's lots of folks named Steve and Robert).

Just remembering everybody's names can be a problem. But what do you expect at my age? There's also Dale, a petite lady from Ocean City, who loves the game and is always ready to play, as well as Ocean City Larry and Lee Duffield, two excellent players.

After a few minutes of warmup and friendly chatter the games usually start by 9:00 as other folks wander in, like Big Tom, a former analyst with Exxon-Mobil who now resides in Egg Harbor Township and Mike James from Cumberland County who gave me the nickname Sneaky Pete. Why? Because I'll make an impossible shot every great once in a while. Mike loves to grow blueberries, and always checks out the height of the nets.

When 10'o clock rolls around, a new group of players arrives. This includes a number of ladies from nearby Ocean City, such as Peg Chernow, Sue Hussong, Nancy Deluisi, as well as Dee, who reminds me of the actress Jean Smart. I cannot forget to mention Lori Conger, an amazing player for her age – don't ask what it is. You never ask a lady her age. It's not polite.

Usually just after 10, with his religious duties completed at the Catholic church in Ocean City, Bill Flanders appears with his friend, Nick. No description of the regulars would be complete without mentioning Bill. He's not the tallest player in the building. What he lacks in height he more than makes up for with speed and agility.

The game we play in Upper is for fun. There is no criticizing a player's skill. Your partner for a game or two is your partner for the length of the game, not a lifetime. It's the "luck of the order." We don't award trophies, we're just happy to be able to get up in the morning and play.

As for myself, I usually finish by 10:15 or so after playing about four games. I try to follow my "Over 75 Rule." Moderation is the key. I still wonder if I'll have an "Over 80 Rule." If I get there.

You can't please all the people all the time.

As the saying goes, "You can't please all the people all the time." The statement rings true not only in politics, which I try and stay clear of, right down to the pickleball court. Thanks to the courtesy of Upper Township, playing pickleball at the community center is free. In addition, most of the folks that play there are great and appreciate the use of the facility.

However. Yes, that wonderful "however" is for the special pickleball players who always want more. For example, we have lightly enforced rules about the number of games people can play in a row if they come early and set up the gym. That number is three, which suits 99% of the players. After 3 games, you put your paddle on the bleachers and wait for the next opening.

To the one percent, especially if they come late, they say it isn't fair. I listen and say, "We'll see what we can do about that." I don't run the program; however, many folks think I do. In my mind I'm thinking, "Why don't you just come earlier, help set up, and then you'll have the opportunity to play three straight games."

When it gets crowded at the facility, usually when there are about a dozen paddles on the bleachers of folks waiting, we'll announce that all new games will be played to a score of 9 rather than 11. That speeds up the games, but it's never enough for the one percent.

To the one percent there's never enough balls, the type of balls, their color, or the portable nets aren't the exact height, and some need repair. As for net repair, I always keep a roll of gaffer tape handy should a center post need fixing. The township does have several new nets available, but we don't want to install them until the ones being used are totally shot.

I can understand complaints if people are paying to play, but a free facility? The one percent should be happy if we let them in the door. If I did run the program, I'd ask them to go someplace else to play, pay, and then they'd have a legitimate reason to complain.

The Pickleball Gypsies

I never imagined I'd be a pickleball gypsy traveling from location to location in search of a place to play. I've played pickleball indoors at the Upper Township Community Center for years.

During that time there was always talk of redoing the floor since time and numerous activities had worn the floor down. Many people weren't aware of the fact that the center was once a candle factory and converted to a recreation center. When funding finally became available to replace the floor and paint the building it was only a matter of time before the center closed for remodeling.

Being the pseudo-organizer for the group, I searched for other places to play even if it was outdoors. The first location I checked out was not far from the community center, off of Marshall Street. There are two tennis courts at the Upper Dog Park. They are lined for pickleball. However, the courts are in bad shape with cracked concrete in numerous places which is a hazard especially to older folks and the nets can't be lowered. That became a quick "No."

Another consideration was Amanda's Field on Route 50. We broached the idea with the township of placing two courts inside the street hockey rink. That was shot down by the public works department.

More determined than ever to find a place to play, I also checked out Caldwell Park in Upper Township. It also has two tennis courts lined for pickleball. Several of us actually played there during the COVID-19 pandemic when the community center was closed. We played there one time. However, the tennis nets couldn't be lowered, and the balls went all over the place. We'd often stop the game just to pick them up.

Not satisfied with Caldwell, I checked out a park at 52nd and Haven Avenue in Ocean City. Someone had drawn two pickleball courts inside the street hockey rink. The original thought was that the walls of the rink would help to reduce the wind. I was wrong on two counts. On our first try only two players showed up, Tom Trainor and me. Plus, the wind was terrible.

Undaunted, I traveled to MK Betterment Park in Egg Harbor Township. It was about a thirty-minute drive which was five to ten minutes more than going to the Upper community center. Following Google's directions, I reached the park without much trouble. After parking I walked over to the courts about 40 yards away. There I gazed upon eight newly built outdoor courts. They were divided into three groups: beginners, intermediate, and advanced. I also saw a number of players I recognized from Upper.

I thought to myself, "If I don't mind the extra few minutes of travel, this would be a good place to play." It wasn't overly crowded and the folks there were friendly. As long as the weather was good, I wouldn't mind playing there until Upper reopened.

Having created an email list of about 21 Upper players to keep them informed about the center's status, I sent out a note suggesting we play at Betterment Park until the center reopened. Over the next week or so several players on the list came to play. They agreed with me that this was a good alternative.

Having found a new place to play, the next problem for me was getting used to playing outdoors. The ball was different and a soft serve, which I often used indoors, didn't make it over the net especially when the wind was blowing in your face. However, lobs still worked if you knew which direction the wind was coming.

Most importantly, we were playing at a great location and could engage in as many games as we wanted without a long wait between matches. Plus, we didn't have to set up the nets or take them down when we were done. It wasn't Upper, but it was a place to play for the time being. And we were no longer gypsies.

Chapter 5: There's No Place Like Home

In the 1938 classic film, *"The Wizard of Oz,"* Judy Garland, playing the role of Dorothy, in her attempt to return to Kansas, repeats the phrase, "There's no place like home. There's no place like home." And, if you live in one home long enough, there is always something to do or redo. This chapter explores some of those doings and re-doings.

A Sign from God

We recently updated our kitchen with new quartz countertops and a backsplash to match. When the company came out to measure for the new tops, they used a laser to measure every nook and cranny. When installed, everything fit perfectly. Once we saw how the countertop looked, we visited different stores to find a backsplash to complement the countertop. At a local store, we found a pattern we liked. We then called a local tile contractor to get an estimate for the job and how much tile we needed for the kitchen walls, including the area under the cabinets and around the room up to the refrigerator.

Based on the estimate and the number of tiles needed to complete the project, we ordered the tiles and other materials required for the project. When the tiles came in, we set up a time for the tile contractor to do the job.

On the day of the installation, two men showed up and went right to work. To do the job correctly, they needed to remove the covers on the electric outlets around the room and pull out the receptacles. The job proceeded smoothly. The tile men were done in a few hours. Before they left, they pushed the receptacles back into the wall and replaced the outlet covers.

After they had gone, I went to turn on the kitchen lights and everything went off, including the refrigerator. It didn't take a genius to figure out there was an electrical problem. My first reaction was to call the tile contractor and ask if they had done something. They told me they hadn't done anything. The one thing I do not like to mess with is electricity. I've been shocked enough in my lifetime trying to fix different electrical problems.

I called my handyman, Jack, to see if he could help us out. Jack answered the phone but was unable to come over. He had projects scheduled all day and was up to his neck in assignments. However, he gave me the names of several electricians he knew in the area that I could try calling to assist us with our problem.

One by one I called the phone numbers he gave me. The phone rang for each, one time, two times, three times, and more. Yet no one picked up on the other end. There was not even an answering machine to leave a message. Not one to give up, I went to the phone book. Yes, I have one of those, and looked up electricians. I selected two in the area and called them with the same result. Either all the electricians were out fishing or at an electricians' convention. Shocking to say the least.

I thought to myself, "This has to be a sign from God." He's telling me I can fix this myself. I immediately grabbed a small screwdriver and removed the cover from the GFI receptacle in the kitchen near the fridge. I then carefully pulled out the unit. Examining the wires behind it, I could see they were touching. I could only assume this occurred when the tile guys pushed the receptacle back into the wall and replaced the cover.

Using my screwdriver, I cautiously separated the wires and made certain they were not touching when I pushed the receptacle back into the wall. I then went to the electrical box in the garage and returned the circuit breaker to the "on" position. It stayed. I then pushed the reset button on the GFI and could hear the refrigerator motor start. Next, I tried the lights. They too went on with no problem. I shook my head, looked upwards, and said, "Thank you, God! You gave me a sign to fix this myself."

Good Stuff Lasts Forever

It's one thing to pass down fine jewelry, like diamond rings, brooches, or necklaces from one generation to another, such as from mother to daughter or to grandchildren when they are old enough. But what about furniture? We've learned that if you purchase good, custom-made furniture, constructed of wood such as cherry, oak, or walnut, and take care of the pieces, they will last for more than 50 years.

When we decided to update our traditionally furnished living room with more of a seashore motif, we offered our formal collection, which included two wing-back chairs, a couch and Pennsylvania House coffee and end tables to our daughter, Laura, who had just purchased a home in Rhode Island.

The chairs and couch were custom made in Telford, PA more than 50 years earlier by a company named Vogel and Finegold. At the time, we traveled to Telford, toured the factory, and selected the coverings. Of course, it took more than three days to build and get delivery, but what is three days versus 50 years of use?

Two years later, after giving the living room furniture to our daughter, our granddaughter, Natalie, announced she was getting married. She heard we were updating our dining area. Natalie asked for the dining room set, which again was about 50 years old and made of burl wood. The set served us well and included several leaves plus 8 chairs. In addition to the table and chairs was a tea cart and credenza. All looking none of 50 plus years of wear and age. Natalie wanted them all.

Divine Reclined Intervention

When we updated our Great Room my favorite piece of new furniture was an electric powered recliner. It allowed me to sit back and relax while watching TV. The recliner replaced a wonderfully comfortable leather chair and ottoman. The chair came with a three-year warranty on the motor.

Almost three-years to the day, the chair malfunctioned. I was watching Jeopardy and was partially reclined in the chair. About half-way through the show, I tried to straighten the   chair to get up and grab a cold drink, but the controls would not work. The chair would only recline further. After getting to a fully reclined position, it was stuck. Nothing would work. I literally had to roll out of the chair. I tried the controls again. Nothing. All I could think of was having this chair fully reclined in the living room for several weeks until a repairman could show up.

As my wife located the receipt for the chair so we could call the furniture store in the morning, I wondered if there was a "You Tube" solution to the problem. I went to my computer and put in "Fixing an electric reclining chair." To my surprise several videos were available.

The first one I viewed had a man telling me to turn the chair over, locate the wiring underneath and trace it to the motor. He then suggested cutting the wires and reattaching them using those typical colored connectors. I thought to myself, "There's no way I'm cutting the wires." I then searched for other solutions on You Tube.

The next video suggested turning the chair over, which weighs about fifty pounds, locating the plug that's connected to the motor and unplugging it for 10 seconds. The presenter then said to turn the chair back over and stated the controls should work. I followed the instructions to a "T", turned the recliner over, unplugged the motor, waited 10 seconds, and returned the chair to the upright position. Again, the chair failed to function.

Checking the video again, the chair needed to be connected to the electrical outlet while performing this task. Undaunted, I followed the steps once again. This time with the chair connected. Again, no luck. I gave it one more attempt. This time I unplugged the chair and unplugged the motor. I waited 10 seconds, then plugged the motor back in and returned the chair to the upright position. I tried the controls once more, again with no success.

Finally, tired of the exercise and repeatedly turning the chair over and over again, I was resigned to calling the furniture store in the morning and trying to get a repair man to service the chair.

The next morning, I got up, went downstairs, and figured I'd try the controls once more, before calling the store. I don't know why, but when I touched the controls, the chair retracked to its normal position and worked perfectly. I don't know how or why. Was it divine intervention?

I Do Believe in Aliens

Ever watch the History Channel and an episode of Ancient Aliens? They've been on for years. Many of the shows feature comments by theorists who believe that ancient aliens came to earth and helped different civilizations around the world advance in everything from astronomy, construction, to mathematics, and more.

Based on a recent home project, I became a true believer. It all began when my wife asked me to redo the carpeting at the top of the steps leading into the garage, as well as the bottom landing which is concrete, using some leftover carpeting. Being one who believes in planning before acting, something I learned from being a Boy Scout, the first thing I did was to determine if I had enough material to complete the job.

I carefully unrolled the leftover remnant from a carpet purchased a few years earlier which I had stored in our shed. I then measured it. To my surprise, it looked like there was enough material. I would hate to get almost done and find out I was short.

With the knowledge that I had enough material to complete the project, I began clearing the boxes and supplies on the landing at the top of the steps. Next, with space to work, I began pulling up the old carpet using a large screwdriver and a pair of pliers, carefully removing the staples that held the carpet in place. There must have been between 40 and 50 staples holding the carpet down. I managed to pull most of them out without getting pinched. But, as luck would have it, the very last staple got me in the finger. And being on a blood thinner, it bled for a while.

Once I had removed the carpet from the top of the steps, I cleaned off the dust and dirt. Then, I took the used carpet outside and laid it on top of the remnant to use as a template for the new covering. Using a sharpie, I marked off the areas to be cut.

With a medium modicum of effort, I created a new piece for the top of the steps. I then laid it into place, and secured it in place with staples, carefully folding the edges around the sides to simulate a professional installation.

After completing the top area, I started working on the bottom landing which is concrete. I removed the well-known brand tape that had held the carpet in place for years, pulled up the piece, and cleaned the area under it. I then took the well-worn piece outside and laid it over the remaining piece of the remnant. I had just enough material to make a new piece for the floor landing. Again, using a sharpie, I marked off the areas to cut and prepared the new piece for where the old one used to lie.

After cutting and trimming the new piece, I put it in place. Since I did not have any of the black tape I had previously used, I applied white tape, but the same brand. However, it did not want to stick to the concrete floor. Undaunted, I went online and researched the best double-sided tape to use on concrete. The suggested tape was a 3M product. I ordered it and it came the next day. Thank you, Amazon! Ready to finish the job, I applied the tape to the bottom of the carpet, removed the second strip of tape and with some pressure attempted to adhere the carpet to the concrete floor. Long story short, it didn't stick.

Pondering my predicament and seeking a solution, I remembered purchasing a box of "Alien Tape," based on an episode of Shark Tank. A guy had invented this tape that would stick to anything, and it was reusable. Although the inventor had died, his daughters presented the product on the show and one of the sharks bought the product outright.

Since I had a box of the product sitting on the shelf, I decided to try it. What did I have to lose? I opened the box, which contained 3 rolls, and cut one strip to size. I adhered it to the concrete floor under where the carpet would sit, removed the top strip of tape, and "voila," it held. With this initial success, I cut several more strips of the magical product and managed to secure the carpet to the concrete floor.

I have no idea what it is made of. All I know is that it works. Based on this success, I used the tape to secure garland outside in freezing weather and for other projects around the house. It holds and leaves no residue when removed. It had to be invented by aliens.

It's Raining Cats and Dogs

Are you familiar with the expression "It's raining cats and dogs." The statement is actually based on fact. During the

Middle Ages, many people lived in thatched-roofed huts with dirt floors. When heavy rains occurred, the peasants placed their animals on the rafters to keep their wet feet from making a mess below. However, when extremely strong storms occurred rain came through the thatched roofs and knocked the cats and dogs off the rafters, thus the expression.

Now, our home in Ocean City is over 20 years old. It doesn't have a thatched roof. It has shingles. I have been told that most roofs last about 30 years, except at the shore. The wind, rain, and salt air can age a roof before its time. Recently I did see some shingles on the ground outside our home. Even my friendly neighbor, Dave Schwartz, was kind enough to bring me pieces he found on his property that looked like those from our roof. With these worn and broken pieces in hand, I came to the realization we needed a new roof, especially when I saw some marks on the ceiling after a three-day rain.

There were several roofing companies in the area, but I had no experience with any of them or their work. So, I started my search by asking neighbors who they had used to replace their roofs, as there are numerous fly-by-night companies and scammers out there.

A neighbor across the alley, also named Dave, recently had his roof replaced. He gave me the name of the roofing company. He and his wife, Lisa, were happy with the job, and only had to call them back once to pick up some materials left on their property. Dave also gave me an idea what the roofing company charged. I knew our price would be different because our roof was quite different from his.

I also talked with friends from the pool to learn who they used to replace their roofs. Roger, originally from Wales, told me he had a repair done by our dental hygienist's husband, Mitch. Mitch had been fixing and installing roofs in the area for years.

Based on Roger's recommendation, we gave Mitch a call. We made an appointment for the next day, and he was there on time. Mitch looked at the roof and agreed it needed replacing. He gave us a verbal estimate for the entire job, as well as one to just repair a section which was leaking. He then said he would follow up with a written estimate in a few days after looking at the roof via Google View.

As promised, Mitch sent us an estimate, detailing his work, the guarantee, and the materials he would use, as well as the price. Our choices were if we wanted the entire roof done or just repaired and what color shingles we wanted. We checked Mitch's company on Facebook. He had high ratings for his fair pricing, quality, and response time in case of problems.

Based on experience, I've learned that it's always prudent to get at least two quotes on a project, especially when you are going to be spending a lot of money. You always wonder if you are getting a good or fair deal.

After receiving the quote from Mitch, we called the roofing company used by my neighbor, Dave. When I called, a young woman answered the phone and was willing to set up an appointment for us. She also wanted to be sure my wife would be home for the session. We finally agreed on a time two days later.

Close to the appointed time, Steve, from the other roofing company, pulled up in a small truck. He introduced himself, took out an adjustable ladder and climbed up on the roof. He was up there for about 20 minutes and then came down.

He put the ladder back in his truck, grabbed a large travel case and came into the house to give us a report of what he found, a demonstration, and a price.

While we were seated at the dining room table, Steve explained his background. He had been a chef but decided to switch careers recently. After the introduction, he took out a laptop computer and showed us a video he had just created featuring our roof and the problems it had, from torn, loose, and missing shingles, to mildew, as well as a host of other problems. He then gave us a presentation featuring his company, the work they do, as well as the Owens Corning (OC) products they use. He impressed upon us that his company was a preferred installer of Owens Corning, and the fact that OC had invented fiberglass shingles.

As he showed us the OC products, he demonstrated how strong and waterproof they were. He even had me drive a nail through some waterproof covering to show how it doesn't leak. Steve then showed us the different layers his company uses on a roof installation. He literally built a model roof on our dining room table.

As we sat there listening, we wondered when he would get to the bottom line, the price for all this wonderful work and materials. So, after 20 minutes we finally said, "What's this going to cost?"

Steve worked on his laptop for a few minutes and then showed us the price for all the goodies he described. It was $10,000 more than Mitch's quote. "That's with everything," he said.

I then responded asking, "Are you replacing the entire roof, including the plywood base?" "No! Just the underlayment and the shingles."

"That's a little high," I said.

"Well, if you don't want everything, here's what we can do."

He then went to the model he had built, still sitting on the table, and removed several pieces.

"If you just want this, we can save you $5000."

He then removed several other pieces from the model and said, "Or we can do the job with these items and save you another $5000." That was still higher than Mitch's original quote.

Seeing the model almost down to the plywood I asked, "For that amount do you just throw a plastic tarp over the roof?"

We then thanked Steve for coming out and giving us a price. He packed up his toys and left. We told him we needed a few days to think things over and would get back to him in a few days as we were getting quotes from several companies.

As you might have guessed, we went with Mitch.

There's Always One More Thing

When my wife inherited some money from her late aunt and uncle in Arizona, she wanted to put part of the funds toward three home-related projects. The first was new railings for the porch and front deck. She had always wanted spindles rather than flat balusters (slats). The second project was new vanities for the three bathrooms as the originals were builder's grade and made of fiberboard rather than wood. The third was new furniture for the dining room, as many of the pieces, though still in good condition, were more than 50 years old.

As you probably know from your own experience, no matter how much you research and plan, few home projects are completed at the estimated price or within the proposed time frame. Think of something along the lines of the 1968 movie *The Money Pit* with Tom Hanks, or the 1948 film *Mr. Blandings Builds his Dream House,* with Cary Grant.

Rather than bore you with details about the good, the bad, and the ugly surrounding the three projects, I'm just going to tell you about just one: the new vanities for the three bathrooms. It was a nightmare that stretched out way beyond the estimated completion time as well as the cost.

This tale actually begins earlier when we replaced our dining room carpet using a local vendor. During our visit to the store, we learned the owner's son had a home remodeling business that focused on kitchens and bathrooms. Since we were very happy with Paul, the owner of the carpet store, we decided to contract with his son, Steve, to replace the vanities. We called Steve and made an appointment with him to come to the house and see the bathrooms.

During his visit Steve took measurements and asked for a few days to draw up designs for each room. A week later we met with Steve at the carpet store. There he presented his ideas for the three bathrooms. My wife liked his suggestions for more space in the master, which included a tower against the wall. We then picked a basic cabinet style and color for all three vanities, which Steve told us could be obtained in a few weeks. We also decided on the same color for the quartz countertops on all three and the same model sink for each vanity.

Steve worked up a price for the project which seemed reasonable and listed the variables. These included the plumbing work and a new mirror for each bathroom. He told us the project could be completed in about 8 weeks. It included removing the large mirrors presently glued to the walls, taking out the existing vanities, installing new ones with the hardware, plus patching the wall in the master bathroom where a medicine cabinet had been.

As for installing the new sinks and related plumbing work, he could supply a plumber at an additional price, or we could have our own contractor perform the work. When it came to the faucets, Steve suggested we purchase them from a plumbing supply house, rather than going to Lowe's or Home Depot. According to him, the faucets would be more expensive but of better quality. We agreed to go with Steve for the project and gave him a deposit for about half. That was in early April.

Relying on Steve's experience, we went to a plumbing supply company in Somers Point. There we selected the faucets and drains for the vanities. Since they also had hardware for the drawers and cabinets, we looked at several types. Terry took down the model numbers of several styles she liked and then checked them out online. She selected the hardware she preferred and gave the information to Steve, who told us he would order it.

Long story short, the 8-week estimate turned into 5 months of frustration and waiting. As many times as we tried to contact Steve for an update, he was never available. Finally, during the first week in August, we heard from him. The cabinets were in the warehouse, and he could send over a crew to remove the existing vanities, the medicine cabinet, and mirrors within the next few days.

The two-man crew, Bob and Bob Jr., was supposed to begin work on a Tuesday morning. They didn't, but showed up the next day, which was par for this project. The removal or deconstruction of the existing vanities included disconnecting the plumbing and taking off the mirrors. It took about a day. We were happy to see that there was tile under each of the original vanities, as the builder seemed to have taken many short cuts when the house was constructed. At least this wasn't one of them.

Since the original mirrors were glued to the walls, I had to repair, sand, and prime the walls behind each once they were removed, as we planned to paint each of the bathrooms as part of the renovation. And, instead of gluing new mirrors to the walls, we would hang them.

The next morning Bob and Bob Jr. appeared and began assembling the new vanities outside and then installed them in each bathroom along with the quartz tops with sinks we had selected. However, they didn't bring the hardware we had ordered for the vanities. Calls to Steve resulted in searches of his warehouse but they couldn't be found. We wondered if he had ever ordered them in the first place. So, we went back to the plumbing supply house and ordered and paid for the hardware ourselves. While there, Terry noticed they had mirrors that matched the new vanities. Though they were several hundred dollars each, we ordered them. Delivery would take 3-6 weeks.

On top of the missing hardware problem, it turned out that the doors to the vanity in the master didn't match. After all the waiting and costs, Terry wasn't going to accept the mistake. She requested Steve order new doors. Knowing how long it took to get the vanities in the first place, we wondered how long replacements would take, but it didn't matter.

Once the new vanities and trim were installed, we faced a new problem and additional costs we hadn't considered.

The new vanities were two inches higher than the originals. They covered part of the electrical outlets in each bathroom. Since I don't mess with electricity, we had to call an electrician to raise the outlets. It took a few days to get an electrician to come out. He did a good job, in spite of the fact that he thought he was coming to install a new light fixture. There was a lack of communication somewhere along the line.

We were able to keep the lighting fixtures in two of the bathrooms as we had previously replaced the original ones. However, the downstairs bathroom required a new fixture. We found one that we liked at Home Depot. However, as hard as I tried, including climbing on the vanity, I was unable to install the new fixture myself as the hole in the wall and the support for the fixture didn't quite match. This required another call to the electrician.

Once the basic installation was completed, we called in a painter we had previously hired, as I wasn't up to painting the three bathrooms myself. We picked the same neutral color for all the rooms. We thought the price was high for the project but gave him the go ahead since he had the time to do the job immediately and we were tired of all the project delays.

To make it easier to paint the downstairs bathroom, we needed to remove the multi-level shelving unit we had in the tub since it was always too small to take a bath. Storage space is always a problem at the shore, and using the tub for storage was a good option. Of course, until you have to move it as well as all the stuff on the shelves.

With the painting completed, we needed to purchase new shower curtains and liners for two of the bathrooms as well as matching toiletries. If you are going to do a project, you might as well do it right. After a few more weeks of waiting, the new door arrived as well as the hardware which Bob and Bob Jr. installed. The job was finally complete, months beyond the original estimate in time and cost. As much as his father was on the ball with the carpeting, we could never recommend Steve to anyone, except maybe my worst enemy, for a remodeling project.

New Feet for Old Socks

I hate to throw anything away even if its time has passed. I know I'm not the only one. When we emptied my in-law's home in South Philadelphia in 2009, we found a rusty old ringer washing machine in the basement from the 1950's, along with shelves from a long-replaced refrigerator.

Before I do throw something out, unless it is really broken, I try and find another use for it. Take for instance sweat socks. I wear crews all the time. When they are stretched and no longer stand up, I used to consider discarding them. However, I've found two new uses that prolong their productive lives.

When I need to change batteries on the smoke detectors on our 12-foot ceilings or clean the ceiling fan blades, it requires the use of a 9-foot ladder which resides in the garage. The rubber feet on the ladder used to leave dark marks on the light-colored carpeting when brought into the house, which then required cleaning. To eliminate the problem, I covered the rubber feet with those old, stretched crew socks which no longer stay on my feet. A little duct tape helps to keep them in place.

Here's also a second use for the old socks. I keep several pairs in the car. They're great for cleaning the side-view mirrors of our cars on wet or snowy days. Once dry, they can be used again and again, thus extending their usual lives beyond the original purpose, and expected lifetime.

Right Time, Right Tool, Right Now

I always like to be prepared for an emergency. Maybe it's based on past experience or having been a Boy Scout. Be it hydrogen peroxide, sterilized wipes, Neosporin, and bandages for cuts and bruises; jumper cables in case of a dead battery, or spare bulbs should a light go out. I think you get the idea. I try to be prepared for everything, well almost everything, within reason.

In my second book, there is a story entitled "Sh-- happens on a Friday night after 5 pm." In it I relate how I had purchased a portable battery-powered wet vac after seeing how my plumber, Tom, used it to unclog an air conditioner drain one Saturday morning.

One afternoon, less than a year later, upon entering the house through the garage, we saw water on the floor. Immediately, we knew the problem: a clogged air conditioner drain. This happens every once in a while, due to the amount of chemicals in our water. They end up blocking the drain. I see this buildup often on the shower heads we use on a daily basis.

Before very much water had soaked the floor (good timing, I guess) I quickly grabbed the little wet vac from my office and went to the rear of the house where the water drains out of a small pipe. A survey of the situation revealed very little water flow coming out of the drain. Having witnessed how the plumber had worked his magic a year earlier, I hooked up the hose of the machine to the pipe in suction mode and turned it on. Within 10 seconds cloudy water and gunk flowed out of the drain and into the tank of the vacuum.

Once the clog was removed the water drained normally and none was coming out of the air conditioning unit. Thankfully, there was no need to call the plumber. Simply stated: Right time, right tool, right now.

Rubber band to the Rescue

I have two hand sprayers that I use from time-to-time for gardening work. The first is a one-gallon Tom Thumb sprayer that I've had for over twenty-five years. It's great for small jobs. The other is a two-gallon model I purchased five years ago for larger projects.

Since my one-gallon sprayer was still full of Neem oil used to treat our holly bushes, I decided to put the larger sprayer to work. I wanted to apply some liquid mace to our plants to prevent the horde of rascally rabbits from eating every flower we had, down to the roots. After I mixed the concentrate with water, I closed the sprayer and attempted to pump it up. As I pushed and pulled on the handle to create pressure, I could hear air escaping from the top of the sprayer. With no pressure I couldn't distribute the mixture. A close examination of the handle yielded a broken two-inch O ring.

Wanting to complete the task without a trip to the hardware store, I decided to try a rubber band as a short-term solution. I took a standard rubber band, about four inches, and doubled it around the location where the O ring would go. Then, I re-screwed the top of the sprayer back into the base and began pumping. To my surprise, the rubber band sealed the unit and enabled me to lay down the mace and save the garden from those herbivorous four-legged pests.

The Mourning Dove Conspiracy

I came across a conspiracy in our town. This one played out right in front of our house, actually on the porch railings and the top of our solar lights. Every day, just as dawn is breaking, the culprits put their plan into action. They seemed to have it timed just right. When I come out in the morning around 7 am, they've gone, but they have left their calling cards, or should I say poop, to let us know they were here.

We have a great many mourning doves in our neighborhood. In the spring they begin building nests anywhere they believe it will be safe from predators. This includes the branches of trees or even a clothespin holder.

Some people enjoy the mournful call of these birds. What I don't enjoy is the mess they leave on our railings and solar lights almost daily. It's no fun cleaning off their droppings every day. If not removed quickly the waste can stain the white vinyl. Since I was getting tired of shooing them away and cleaning up after them, I came up with a safe hack that seems to be working.

After cleaning the railings and the tops of the solar lights, I wiped them down with a cloth soaked in household-strength ammonia. Apparently, the strong smell of the potion acts as a deterrent but doesn't harm the birds. It just keeps them away, at least from my place, and throws a wrench in their daily conspiracy.

Wascally Wabbits

Who can forget watching Bugs Bunny and Elmer Fudd in Looney Tune Cartoons at the movie theater on Saturday afternoons and then on television. That pesky rabbit was always finding a way to beat Mr. Fudd. We laughed as kids, but as adults tending to our gardens full of flowers and vegetable plants, it isn't very funny when Bugs and his friends are in the area.

Ocean City has an abundance of rabbits. They're everywhere on the island. In addition to Bugs' favorite, carrots, they eat almost everything they can find in flower beds and vegetable gardens, including tiger lilies, holly bushes, mums, and pepper plants. You name it and there's a ninety percent chance they'll eat it, especially if they're hungry. In addition to their appetite, they reproduce like, like rabbits.

My neighbors and I have tried many things to protect our plants. We've used cayenne pepper, human hair, and a

169

number of products on the market, such as deer and rabbit repellent spray, granules and mace, solar repellents, as well as fencing. I even had a neighbor trap and transport the culprits to a nearby nature preserve. However, they or their relatives always find a way back and take revenge. It seems they know a good thing and like to eat it.

Recently, I was looking through a current issue of a gardening/handyman catalog called "Whatever Works," to see if there were any new products of interest to me. One that caught my eye was called The Cat Scat Mat. The description said the mat could prevent animals from digging in your garden and potted plants. In addition, it could keep them away from areas to be protected, like your yard, and around trees.

The narrative further stated that it was a humanized b solution and did not contain any chemicals or toxins. "Animals will feel uncomfortable when they step on the mat, but it will not hurt them at all. The mat was made of high-quality plastic and could be bent freely. In addition, the mats were suitable for any environment, easy to use, and could be easily cut into any shape as needed to fit any space."

Thinking of my garden, this looked like a great non-violent solution. I ordered a box. It came with 12 pieces plus several garden staples, as well as plastic ties to hold the mats in position.

Upon arrival, knowing I was in a battle with pesky critters, I quickly went to my garden and cut several of the mats into four by eight-inch pieces to surround my most precious flowers and plants. I anchored the mats in place, using the garden staples.

It's been several weeks into the experiment and no plants surrounded by the mats have been devoured or flowers eaten. I'm cautiously optimistic. And, I can honestly say that no rabbits were harmed during the writing of this story.

What, Me Worry?

Remember the slogan of Alfred E. Neuman, the fictitious mascot and cover boy of Mad Magazine? It was "What, Me Worry?" If you decide to purchase an extended warranty for a car or appliance, should you worry about repairs or replacement? I wonder.

Buying an extended warranty for a car or household appliance is always an interesting decision. Should we or should we not purchase one? We often ask ourselves, "What is the expected lifetime time of the item? Will a repair cost us more than a new one?" Remember when Maytag used to promote the quality of their washers and dryers with the bored repairman? We had a Maytag laundry pair for 23 years and never needed a repair. In fact, when we moved, both appliances were still in working condition.

Television is full of extended warranty commercials for both cars and appliances. The water company offers warranties covering our outside pipes to and from the house, as well as inside plumbing problems. The gas company offers them for heating and air conditioning. The electric company is also in the warranty business. You could go broke if you took advantage of every one of them. Our homeowner's policy actually covers breakage of the water lines into and out of our home. Maybe yours does also? Check your coverage.

I'm generally not into buying extended warranties. Our auto insurance company offers the option of warranty-like coverage on new cars for up to seven years or so many thousands of miles with a deductible. We don't put that many miles on our cars anymore and don't usually keep our vehicles for more than seven years. So, that works for us. My wife is the perfect example of a lady who just drives her car to church and back.

Several years ago, for some reason, we took out an extended warranty for our electric range. My wife wanted electric rather than gas because she felt it was better for baking, which she does often. She would actually rather bake than cook. When the initial warranty on the appliance was up, we took the extended service plan. It was just over one hundred dollars for three years. We felt it was worth it since the plan covered parts and service. Out of habit, we just kept renewing the plan every three years. Before we knew it the range was eleven years old.

This year, after continuing the warranty for another three years, we needed to use it. One of the elements on the cooktop would not shut off. I tried the button on the control panel. Nothing happened. I then switched off the breaker in the garage and waited ten minutes and then flipped it on again. The element still wouldn't shut off. For safety reasons, I again turned the range off at the breaker.

Next, I searched for the warranty document and called the number listed on the policy. After a 45-minute wait, I finally reached Henry, a live person, explained the problem, and gave him the serial number on the range, as well as the policy number.

After a short wait, Henry provided us with a repair code and also contacted a repair company to set up an appointment for them to perform the service. I was anticipating that he was going to give us the repair department of the company where we originally purchased the appliance, but he didn't. You see that company doesn't carry parts for appliances more than 10 years old. This was beyond that time period.

Henry was able to make us a service appointment for two days later. He also gave us a choice of times, morning, or afternoon. We accepted the morning appointment.

On the appointed day, we received a call from the repairman at about 9:35 am. He was only ten minutes away and would be there shortly. He also asked if the burner was off. If it was on, it would be too hot to work on. We assured him it was off.

The repairman, Bruce, arrived a few minutes later and went right to work. He quickly disassembled the stove top and replaced the malfunctioning element. After reassembling the cooktop, he asked me to turn the breaker back on. I did and the misbehaving element immediately lit up like a Christmas tree. Bruce quickly deduced that the circuit board was the problem. Several thoughts ran through my mind, "What would it have cost us for a service call and the parts if we didn't have a warranty? How much would a new oven cost us if they can't get the board? How long would we have to wait for a new oven?"

To our surprise, Bruce said that he could order the board, but it would take a week to ten days. When it came in his company would set up another appointment to install it. We said "Okay." We'd just have to live without the range for another 10 days. We'd tried to make do with an electric frying pan and a toaster oven.

A few days later, our neighbor, Sam, who has a farm in Mickleton, NJ, gave us several fresh zucchinis. Being a baker, not wanting to have the zucchinis go to waste, and having a great recipe, my wife wanted to turn them into zucchini bread. She asked me if I thought we could still use the oven to make the bread. I told her that the element would go on when we threw the breaker, but if we were careful, she might be able to accomplish her goal.

After she cut up the zucchinis, mixed the ingredients, and placed them into several tin pans, I turned on the range from the breaker. The oven worked and the element turned on, as expected. My wife quickly placed the tins into the oven and set the timer. However, before ten minutes had passed, the fan on the microwave above the range went off. This was a warning sign to stop and turn off the oven.

Not wanting to waste her efforts, she removed the half-baked pans from the oven and placed them in the toaster oven. As luck would have it all the zucchini breads turned out fine. Each loaf was moist and tasty.

A week later, on a Thursday afternoon, the repair company called. They had the new circuit board and set up an appointment to install it on Monday of the following week. As he had done previously, Bruce called us when he was on his way with the new part. He said he'd be there in 30 minutes, and he was.

Upon his arrival, Bruce went straight to work. He pulled the range out from the wall, disassembled the control panel and installed the new board in less than an hour. Once the installation was complete, Bruce instructed me to flip the breaker on. Instantly the range came to life. He tested the controls and made certain each element could be turned on and off. My wife was back in business. This was one warranty I didn't need to worry about. And just think, it's still in effect for another three years.

Chapter 6: Everything, Anything, One at a time

Like the title states, this chapter contains a little bit of everything, including events I have lived through, some imagination, strange occurrences, the unexplained, as well as helpful memoir writing tips.

Christmas Cookies for Virginia

Do you remember the story or the movie about the response to a letter, "Yes, Virginia there is a Santa Claus." It was when eight-year-old Virginia O'Hanlon sent a letter to the New York Sun asking, "Please tell me the truth; is there a Santa Claus?" The newspaper's editor handed it to Francis Church, a veteran Sun writer for the famous reply.

Though I'm Jewish, I do play St. Nick at Christmas time. While I was working, I shipped or hand-delivered Christmas treats to business associates, friends, my siblings, and favorite physicians. It was something my father, Louie, taught me. I liked and enjoyed doing it in appreciation of our relationship.

When I retired, my gift list became shorter. It included close friends, my two siblings and some of my favorite doctors. You have to keep those docs happy. As you age, you get to know more doctors.

My older sister, Betsy, usually received a box of chocolate-coated saltwater taffy from Shiver's in Ocean City as a remembrance of the times we spent at the seashore as youngsters. Other folks on my short list received boxes containing 12 of Shriver's famous macaroons; six coconut and six almond. Having sent these same sweet treats year after year, many of the recipients became addicted to them. Upon arrival many quickly gobble their dozen.

However, this past Christmas, my longtime friend, Larry Stein, made a special request. He and his wife, Angela, had moved to the middle of nowhere in central Virginia.

Apparently, there are no real family bakeries within a hundred miles (we don't include Walmart or supermarket bakeries). Larry and Angela had a hankering for real Christmas cookies and couldn't find any.

Knowing my wife is an excellent baker (She'd rather bake than cook) and loves to make a wide variety of cookies at Christmas including pecan balls, log jams, and spritz cookies, they put in a request for the following year. "Forget the macaroons. Just send us homemade Christmas cookies next year," said Larry.

As luck would have it, since Terry bakes large quantities, we had a generous supply of the goodies still inhouse. Wanting to make their holiday this year a joyous one, we carefully boxed the treats and shipped them priority mail.

Two days later we got the call, "Yes, there were Christmas cookies in Virginia."

My High School Reunions

Unlike *Romy and Michele's 10th High School Reunion* where two 28-year-old girls who appear to have not achieved much success in life, decide to invent fake careers to impress former classmates, or *Peggy Sue Got Married*, or even *Grosse Point Blank*, mine was a blur since I didn't have much to do with it except attend with my wife. What I do remember most was that if someone was an "a-hole" in high school, there was a good chance they were still an a-hole at the 10th, 25th and even the 50th. Attendance did not prove me wrong.

High school reunions are supposed to be fun experiences or chances to relive the past, like many incorporated into movies on the Hallmark channel where they all end with a kiss – a Hallmark movie trademark.

I still remember a conversation with my late mentor, Val Udell, about his high school reunions from Gratz High School in Philadelphia. Val was one of the last surviving members of his class. After all these years he was still engaged in a vigorous dispute with the treasurer on how the money for it was being spent and what to do with the remaining funds. I think there were only 10 members alive at last count. Whatever!

I've been to three "formal" reunion events for our graduating class of January 1963. The first was our 10-year. The second was the 25th and the third was our 50th. Was there a formal 60th? The answer is "No." The 60th was a luncheon at Johnny's, a restaurant in Margate, New Jersey, where several of the original reunion organizers now reside. There were only eleven attendees as several classmates declined at the last minute for medical reasons. Others just weren't interested in coming. However, on the same day, a general Olney High reunion was held at Ann's Choice in Pennsylvania. According to reports it was attended by about 65 former graduates, but only one from our class, Sue Melhorn.

As I noted earlier, I honestly don't remember too much about the 10th reunion. It was a busy time: raising a family, making a living, and just existing in the early 1970's. However, I know I was there. I can remember a dark room and the late Barbara Herring, who suffered from MS, coming via a wheelchair. That was something that has always stuck in my mind.

Nevertheless, I did get involved in the planning of the 25th, which was held at the Cedarbrook Country Club, just outside of Philly in 1988. I went to several meetings at Carole (Horowitz) Ziev's home and helped with the "Memory Book." The tome provided the latest contact and career information about the attendees. It also included a memorial to the several classmates who had passed since our graduation. Being in the audiovisual business, I created a 35mm slide presentation about our high school and class using pictures from the yearbook.

Having assisted with the 25th and remaining in contact with several of the planners of that event, I was asked if I wanted to help with the 50th. I said, "Yes!" My involvement with this event included designing and developing the invitations with the assistance of my classmate and friend Larry Stein. I also created a humorous health questionnaire for all attendees. In addition, I constructed a form to collect data for the assembly and printing of a memory book containing the latest information about members of the class.

To announce the 50th, which was being held on May 5th, 2013, and develop the memory book, we sent invitations to classmates we had addresses for. It included the date of the event, cost for attending per person, as well as a form requesting career and family information about the classmate.

Led by Ruthi (Scholnick) Eckelman, the organizing committee, which included myself as well as Cooky (Rothenberg) Gross, Joy (Salus) Scholnick, Sandy (Silver) Hersh, Arlene (Weisberg) Shuster) and Walt Spector did a great job. The event was held on a bright sunny day at the Mansion House in Voorhees, New Jersey.

More than sixty-five members of the class attended along with spouses and/or partners. Some folks looked the same, just a little older. Others were a little more difficult to recognize. It was either due to rapid aging or in some cases a little plastic surgery.

At this point in time, I can't tell if there will be another gathering of the Class of January 1963, like a 65th or 70th. Who knows? Who will be around? Who will run it? All I know is I hope they pick a different restaurant.

My Sister Bugs Me

This story is based on an incident that occurred years ago while I was growing up in Philadelphia. As much as you may like your brother or sister, there are times when things aren't perfect. This was one of those instances.

It all began on a summer day in the late 1950's. The sturdy buttonwood trees on the curbs of Georgian Road swayed in a warm gentle wind. The pesky pigeons were nestled on the rooftops of the brick row homes. It was on such a peaceful afternoon that I was sunbathing on the patio reading *The Catcher in The Rye*.

Suddenly, my reverie was interrupted by a shrill cry, "Help! Pete, help!"

I marked the page I was reading, put the book down on the chaise, sprang to my feet, ran up the front steps, and entered the house.

"Help! Pete, help!" came the cry again. It was coming from the second floor. Up the stairs I ran following a trail of broken shampoo and perfume bottles and scattered shoes to the bathroom where my eyes fell upon a small, defenseless creature in the corner of the bathroom. It was a cockroach. I could tell by its reddish-brown color and six skinny legs.

My sister, standing on top of the sink, as far away as possible, was a bit shaken but by no means small or defenseless.

"Kill it!" she cried. "Kill it! It's ugly."

I felt like saying, "So what! So are you." and going back to my novel. But I had to do something, or my sister would tell my father and I'd never hear the end of it.

"Step on it! Step on it!" she yelled.

"I can't," I said. "I don't have any shoes on." "Well, go get one and quick," she ordered.

I turned and walked down the hall to my room. Then I went to the closet and started checking my shoe rack.

"Should I use a sneaker? No, I don't want to get the bottom dirty. One of my new loafers won't do either."

Just then I saw the perfect thing, an old combat boot. Back to the bathroom I marched armed with the big, old boot. My sister was still on top of the sink and the little roach was still in its corner.

"Well, what are you waiting for now?" she asked. "Kill it!" I looked at the poor defenseless creature (the roach, not my sister).

"The heck with you! I've got nothing against this bug. Do it yourself," I said.

With that I threw the boot to the ground. It bounced and landed on the insect with a squish. The roach was still moving, but it was dying. I felt sorry for the critter and decided to put it out of its misery.

I picked up the boot and started hammering away, but the roach's legs kept moving. At last, the legs stopped.

"Now clean it up!" ordered my sister.

"I'll fix her wagon," I thought.

That evening I went to the hobby shop and bought a giant model of a honeybee. I worked all night to assemble it. When it was completed, the insect measured eleven inches in length and had an eighteen-inch wingspan. Now the question was how to use the plastic monster.

I decided to put it in my sister's room while she was asleep. I quietly placed the bee on her bureau and went to bed with the hope that dawn and revenge were not far away.

At 7:00 am came the reckoning. "Eck! Help! Crash!" were the sounds that came from my sister's room. Everyone came running to her room.

"What's wrong?" I asked innocently.

"That!" cried my sister pointing to the broken bee on the floor.

"Oh, I just wanted to show it to you, but you were sleeping. So, I left it in your room."

"Don't ever do that again," said my father, who was now at the scene of the crime.

My sister felt sorry for breaking the bee and even gave me the money to buy a new model, but I went out and bought an alligator.

The Resurrection

Belief in the resurrection is central to Christianity. It shows that Jesus defeated death, and it is considered by many Christians to be proof of life after death. My wife attends church six days week, is a eucharistic minister, and takes part in weekly bible discussions.

In addition, three days a week she delivers holy communion to elderly parishioners who are unable to attend church. One lady in particular appears to be my wife's favorite. Her name is Eileen. She is ninety-seven, gave birth to thirteen children, and still has her marbles. When my wife goes to

Eileen's home in the Gardens section of Ocean City, she usually stays a while and chats with Eileen. My wife's favorite seat while at Eileen's is an old wooden rocker, probably as old as the lady herself.

On one of her visits, my wife noticed the rocker was nowhere in sight. When she asked Eileen's aide, Cece, about it, she learned it was broken. The seat had split and several of the supporting spindles on the base frame were out of their holes making it dangerous to sit on. However, it hadn't been thrown away and was placed in another room. That's when this resurrection began.

My wife asked me if I could fix the chair. I told her I wasn't sure. I hadn't seen it and didn't know what condition it was in. I asked her to take some photos of the chair using her cell phone on her next visit so I could assess what needed to be done and to determine if it could be saved.

Three days later, on her next communion run to Eileen's, she took several photos. Based on a careful examination of the pictures, I could see the seat was definitely split down the middle and would need to be braced in several places if it was ever to safely hold a person again.

The following afternoon I made a trip to a nearby hardware store to see what they had in metal supports that I could use to resurrect the chair and bring it "back to life." Basically, I was winging it. I knew what I wanted to accomplish but wasn't sure what the store had that I could use.

With a determined spirit looking over my shoulder, I searched through a wide variety of metal braces, changing my mind several times. I finally decided on 3 nine-inch metal straps, each about an inch wide. To secure them in place, I purchased a box of 8 x ¾ screws, along with a bottle of wood glue just in case. The entire cost of the materials was under $23 dollars.

That Sabbath morning, with the newly purchased supplies in hand, along with my battery powered drill, and an assortment of extra screws (just in case), my wife and I went to Eileen's. Upon our arrival I located the broken chair and brought it into the living room, where I could examine it first-hand and perform the repair.

The seat was definitely split as shown in the photos. In addition, several of the base frame struts were out of position. With the task assessed and a solution in mind, I started the resurrection by turning the chair over. I then placed some wood glue on the ends of the base struts and pushed them into their normal position which gave support to the chair's feet and allowed it to safely rock.

With the base stabilized, I then started work on the seat. I strategically placed the three metal straps across the bottom to determine where they would give it the most support. I then marked the position of each strap with a pencil, as well as where I could place the screws to hold the straps in place.

Using my drill, I made starter holes for each of the screws. I then secured the three straps in position with the 8 x ¾ screws making sure none of the points came through the seat base, as they would pinch the cheeks of anyone sitting in the chair. Once all the screws were in place, I followed up with a strip of wood glue along the seam of the original split in the seat.

After setting the chair upright, I told Eileen not to allow anyone to sit in the chair for a day, as the glue needed to thoroughly dry. I then packed up my tools and prepared to leave. Eileen thanked me for my work, as did my wife. The chair was once again functional and starting the following week it would give my wife a comfortable place to sit, pray, and deliver communion to Eileen.

Roger and Mariah

One of my friends, Roger, was a professional sailor for many years. In the course of his ventures at sea, he often came in contact with Mariah. She helped to guide his boat wherever he went. However, on one of his voyages, he met a lady named Kate and married her. They eventually moved to Ocean City which is where I first met them.

Looking for a home with no steps, Roger and Kate recently moved to a rancher in Linwood, NJ. Roger is very meticulous as well as handy. Skills he learned from life on the water. Like me, he loves to garden. Unlike me, he starts many of his crops from seed. I, on the other hand, like to purchase plants that are already started. Plus, since I have a smaller garden area, I limit what I grow to tomatoes and basil, plus some cold weather veggies in a raised bed to elude the rabbits. But enough about me.

Since Roger has more gardening space at his new home, he purchased a small greenhouse from Walmart to start his plants from seed. He quickly assembled the structure and placed it on his patio. The greenhouse came with a number of starter trays. As is his style, Roger carefully labeled each row in the trays as he carefully placed seeds in them on the shelves in the greenhouse.

However, shortly afterwards, Roger had an unexpected run-in with Mariah. If you are familiar with the musical, *Paint Your Wagon*, there's a song about Mariah. It goes something like this "Way out here they have a name for rain and wind and fire. The rain is Jack, the Fire is Joe, and they call the wind Mariah. Mariah blows the stars around...

Well, Mariah, apparently unhappy with Roger having left the seafaring life, took her revenge. It happened soon after Roger had finished assembling his greenhouse and placing his seed trays in it. With one good gust, followed by another, Mariah quickly blew his greenhouse around and scattered the seeds and trays everywhere.

After the incident, Roger moved his greenhouse off the patio and anchored it into the ground. However, his seeds and trays were scattered to the degree that he couldn't tell what seeds went where or what they would grow into. All he could do was wait until the seedlings grew and discover what kind of salad Mariah had created for him.

Groundhog Week

Who hasn't seen the film *Groundhog Day* with Bill Murray at least once? It's shown repeatedly on February 2nd, Groundhog Day, when Punxsutawney Phil is supposed to see his shadow and let folks know how many more weeks of winter there will be.

Bill, playing the role of a narcissistic, self-centered TV weatherman, finds himself in a time loop. While covering the yearly event, he relives the day, day after day, until he gets it right. We can only guess how many times. During his daily repeat, Bill saves a boy falling out of a tree, changes a flat tire for some elderly ladies, saves a man from choking, buys insurance from a past acquaintance and learns how to play the piano. It could have been months of Groundhog Days. Think how long it really takes to learn to play the piano.

I recently had an experience that I thought was going to be Groundhog week. Here's the story. Though retired I still use a 2-page daily planner to keep track of my activities and what I want to accomplish each day. Over the years I've purchased planners from a variety of companies, including Day-Timers, for whom I did some work in the late 1990's, as well as FranklinCovey, and At-A-Glance. I usually purchase the planner I can get for the best price.

I always put the planner pages in my looseleaf binder, one month at a time, as each month arrives. All things went well until March. Believing all the correct pages were there, I began entering future events, like doctors' appointments, and meetings.

When I turned to the page to list a scheduled meeting on the 28th, I noticed there was no page for that date. Where there should have been the two pages for Tuesday the 28th, I saw

Monday, March 20th. A review of the planner pages showed everything from the second page of March 26th as incorrect. What should have been March 26th was the second page of March 18th. From that page on, it was a repeat of the planner pages for March 19th thru March 26th, with no second page for that date.

I pondered what to do. I thought if I kept those pages as they were I might have to relive March 19th through the 26th again until the first of April, skipping half of March 19th. Thinking of the film, I wondered what I could improve upon or alter in a "do over" for a week I hadn't even lived yet. Would I say something different to the cashier at ShopRite? Would some items be back on special that week? Could I improve a relationship with a person I hadn't met yet or repair something that hadn't even broken? How about learning to play the piano? Nah! That wasn't me. Of course, I could have just renumbered the pages and days of the week in the planner, as they were different from the missing ones. I attempted that but it looked sloppy.

Not satisfied with my fix, I searched online for the phone number of the company that made the planner, as I had purchased it through Amazon and didn't believe I could get a real person there to assist me. I was able to find the firm's 800 number and called. After going through a level of menu choices, I reached a "live" body and informed the man of my problem. When I told him I had purchased the product from Amazon, he switched me over to another department. This time a woman answered the phone with the name of a different but well-known supplier of planners.

I once again explained about the missing pages. She seemed familiar with the problem. Apparently, I wasn't the only person affected by what appeared to be a production problem. Long story short, they didn't have my model planner in stock to send me the missing pages. There must have been a ton of people before me who called about the problem. How many folks want to relive a week without knowing what could happen? When I mentioned the film *Groundhog Day* she laughed.

But that's not the end of the story. The company was supposed to ship me a completely new set of 2-day planners via FedEx for the year, similar to the one I had purchased. A week later it had not appeared. Thinking the worst, I called the company once more. After repeatedly going through numerous menus, I finally reached a live person. I once again repeated my tale of the missing pages and the promise of receiving a new set. After an exhaustive search, the lady was unable to find any information about my earlier call or an order to my home address.

Wanting to provide good customer service, she said she would research the company's database with her manager and give me a call back as she didn't want me just hanging on the phone. I gave her my number and within 30 minutes my call was returned. The company wanted to make me happy and offered to send a new set. This time I had a choice. I could get of complete set of this year's planner or wait a week and get a set for next year.

I decided to take the company up on their offer for a set of next year's planner, as I didn't want to start from the beginning and relive the whole year over again.

I can see Italy from my backyard.

Do you remember when Sarah Palin, a former governor of Alaska and vice-presidential running mate for John McCann, told the world, "I can see Russia from my backyard." And people laughed. I have a friend, Dan DeSantis, who can make a similar claim. Not about seeing Russia from his back porch, but Italy. Here's the story.

Dan moved to a suburb of Williamsburg, VA about 22 years ago. He built a new home there and over time made numerous additions to his property, many completed with his own hands. Dan liked to describe his efforts as "having sweat equity" in the work.

Not wanting to really look into the backyards of his two neighbors or they into his, Dan wanted to build a fence. Not just any fence. He called six different fence companies before he found one that would build it to his specifications. The end result was an eight-foot high, white vinyl fence with a two-foot lattice topping across his 200-foot rear property line. This gave Dan a ten-foot barrier between him and the folks behind him.

Dan now had his privacy, but he wasn't finished. Several years earlier, in 2016, Dan had come across a beautiful picture of an Italian villa on his page-a-day calendar. He had said to himself at the time, "Someday I'm going to use this picture," and saved it. When the fence was completed, Dan now had the perfect canvas for his villa picture that he had dreamed about using for years. All he had to do was figure out how to blend the two. It was a challenge Dan was up for.

First, he went online, and with some searching, found the villa picture. He secured the rights to it for $12.00. That was the easy part. Then he needed someone to help fulfill his vision. He wanted a full-color wrap made of the picture adhered to three 5' x 10' panels that could be attached to the vinyl fence. As luck would have it, Dan found a local sign/graphics company willing to fulfill his dream.

After several weeks of waiting, the panels were completed and affixed to the fence. The finished size was 10 feet high and 15 feet long. Dan then planted Carolina Jasmine around it as a frame. He now could look out from his back porch and see a little bit of Italy every day.

When I asked Dan how much it cost for the fence and the wrap, he said about $25,000.00. For that much, he probably could have easily taken a trip to Italy and seen the real villa. But that wasn't Dan.

Bloody Christmas

Unlike the character Jack Skellington in Tim Burton's *Nightmare before Christmas*, who tried to improve Christmas, my wife knows exactly how it should be done and always has a plan.

We have been married for more than half a century. Christmas is by far Terry's favorite holiday of the year, hands down. Our attic is filled with large plastic containers and boxes full of holiday decorations. You name it, we have it. There are containers for lights, balls, linens, outside garland, tablecloths, pillows, and trains. And how could I forget swags for the windowsills? I think you get the picture.

At Thanksgiving, which we always host, our grown sons bring down the Christmas armada from the attic and stack the containers in a spare bedroom.

Usually around the first week of December, on a warm day, we'll start decorating outside. For years this included attaching several 9-foot, battery-powered lighted garland strands to the railings on the upstairs front deck, as well as on the porch and over the front door.

We always drape the railings first with clear plastic. This keeps the garland from staining the rails. We fasten the plastic and the garland to the rails with 15-inch zip ties.

Years ago, we cut the plastic to size and marked each piece as to its length and where it went. Over time the original plastic became stained and the marks indicating the location were blurred. It then became a game of mix and match to get the plastic to fit.

While Terry knew what we wanted to accomplish, each year, as we grew older, the task became a little harder. The smart approach was to pick a day with little or no wind, and to wear gloves as the garland was rough on your hands and bent from being stored in containers for almost a year.

This past year I made one mistake as we started to put up the garland. I forgot to wear a pair of gloves. As my wife was securing the garland in place, I was lining it up with the rails. With a small gust of wind, the garland turned. As I grabbed hold to keep it straight, a strand "bit" me. The result was a cut on the backside of my left hand. As I am on blood thinners, it was quite a mess. We went inside, cleaned the cut, and put a band aid over it. We then finished putting up the garland. That was not the end of the story.

A few days later, thinking the cut had healed, I went to remove the band aid. As I did, the adhesive from band aid took a piece of skin with it, and I bled all over the place. What did you expect from an old Jewish guy hanging Christmas garland?

Divine Providence

Traditional theism holds that God is the creator of heaven and earth, and that all that occurs in the universe takes place under Divine Providence — that is, under God's sovereign guidance and control. So, what happened to my wife and I one night in the city of Providence was possibly just that. What we did to deserve it, I just don't know.

Remember when a well-known national hotel chain had the slogan, "Our sign stands for quality, or it doesn't stand at all." I think our one-night stay at their facility in Providence, Rhode Island back in 1998 was the reason they changed it.

At the time, our daughter, Laura, was a student at the Rhode Island School of Design (RISD). She was having an a one-person exhibition of her work at the school for only a single night.

My wife and I planned to drive up from New Jersey to attend the reception which began at 6:30 pm.

A week in advance, I called and made a reservation for that one night. I was quoted a rate of approximately $95 for two people with a queen bed in a non-smoking room. When I mentioned I had an Entertainment Card Book, one of those promotional books kids sell for fund raising, I was quoted the discounted rate of $65. Thirty bucks less for the same room and having a kid in college that was a savings. So, I booked the room.

We reached the hotel at approximately 5:45 pm and checked in. When we entered our room, we saw that it had a full bed, not the queen we had requested. Being tired from the five-plus hour drive, and knowing we had to get to the reception, we figured it was only one night and could put up with it. That was the first disappointment we encountered.

Off we went to the reception which was only a few blocks away. We returned to the room the room at about 10 pm, ready for a good night's sleep. That was then that we were faced with a second disappointment. Upon close examination, as we brushed our teeth and prepared for bed, we discovered the bathroom was moldy. This completely turned off my wife, who was born with a clean gene. "This will never do!" she said. I reminded her that it was only one night, and we could live through it.

Then the phone rang once. I picked it up. No one was on the other end. That was our third disappointment. The phone continued to ring once, almost every hour throughout the night, 11 pm, 12am, 1am, all night long, until morning.

The "good times" just kept on coming. When we went to close the drapes to darken the room, we found that only the shears would close, not the heavier drapes. There was no way to darken the room. But the best of all was the bed itself. Once in it, the mattress cover curled up around us, not only from my wife's side, but from my side also. Try sleeping with a mattress cover wrapping around you.

When morning thankfully arrived, we checked out. Before leaving, I mentioned our problems to the desk clerk. She only seemed concerned about the mattress pad and getting that fixed. There was no apology or anything. We crossed that hotel off of our list of habitable places, vowing to never to stay there again, even if they gave us a free night. Providence was certainly not divine to us that night.

We returned to Providence several times after that to attend parents' weekends and graduation. For those stays we chose another well-known hotel. It didn't have a discounted rate, but it wasn't a discounted room either.

Not exactly Stanley and Dr. Livingstone

Ever heard of Henry M. Stanley and his search for the long, lost Dr. David Livingstone in darkest Africa during the late 1870's? It was a great adventure story of the human spirit and perseverance turned into a wonderful film starring Spencer Tracy. Stanley eventually did find the great humanitarian and continued his work.

However, my search for a friend and colleague was not so successful and it wasn't in Africa. Let me start at the beginning. Networking is an important part of freelancing which is what I did for most of my career. When I first began working as a freelance instructional designer (ID) in the 1990's, to get to know more people, as well as to learn about job opportunities, I joined the Greater Philadelphia chapter of The American Society for Training and Development (ASTD).

Many of their monthly meetings were held in Conshohocken. It was at one of these gatherings that I first met a fellow employed by Merck in brand training. I would run into him from time to time at different organization meetings. Saying "hello" and chatting about work was the extent of our relationship.

Several years later, I ran into him again at a pharmaceutical meeting in North Jersey. He was now working for a company based in New York City. When we met in the parking lot after the meeting it was like two old friends having a reunion. We exchanged numbers and promised to talk more often.

Over the next few years, I worked on numerous healthcare projects with him. When he needed a creative idea for a workshop, we would brainstorm and come up with several approaches to meet his client's needs. We even met for lunch a few times.

When he switched jobs and moved over to another company, we continued our collaboration. If he needed some different approaches for a workshop or an e-learning program, I was happy to offer creative suggestions. Sometimes I was hired to develop the project itself. After several years at this organization, and as the economy tightened, new projects became fewer, and my friend was eventually let go from his job.

In an effort to help him find a new source of income, I provided leads for freelance work, which is how I made my living. However, he was different from me and looking for full time employment – a steady paycheck, as his wife had fallen ill, and he needed benefits.

Eventually, he landed an ID position with a company in Pennsylvania. They allowed him to work from home as his wife's illness worsened. After his wife's passing, we talked for several months, then the lines of communication went silent. He didn't answer my phone calls, messages, or emails. The yearly desktop calendar I sent to folks, even after I retired, came back as undeliverable.

As I considered him a friend, I wanted to stay in touch, but he seemed to have disappeared. Being persistent, as is my nature, I tried reaching out to the last company where he had worked. However, I was never able to get to a live person or an operator, especially during the pandemic.

Tapping all possible avenues of contact, I asked a longtime friend who worked on different projects for that same company, to see if she could uncover his whereabouts. According to her project manager, the man still worked for the company. My longtime friend even sent him an email at the address given to her by the manager. There was no response. I did the same with a similar response. Nothing.

This experience has been a little strange for me as I still remain in contact with friends from as far back as kindergarten and high school. In addition to those folks, I retain friendships with a number of creative colleagues from my years of developing training programs. Sometimes the contact is an email, a joke, or just a phone call. The purpose: to chat, wish each other happy birthday, or to offer congratulations for some milestone. For me it's a great way of keeping the lines of communication open as friendships are something I hold dear.

Will the Blob Return?

Ever watch the low budget science fiction classic *"The Blob"*? A drive-in favorite for many years, the film followed teenagers Steve (Steven McQueen in one of his first films) and his best girl, Jane, as they tried to protect their hometown from a gelatinous alien life form that engulfed everything it touched. The first to discover the substance and live to tell about it, Steve and Jane witnessed the blob destroying an elderly man and grow to a terrifying size. But no one else had seen the goo, and the police refused to believe the kids without proof.

The mass of carnivorous jell from outer space terrorized and feasted on a host of folks from Phoenixville, PA. Networks often show the film at Halloween or during a horror film festival. There's even a yearly *Blobfest in Phoenixville. It's* a 3-day event that commemorates the classic 1958 movie that had a famous scene filmed at the Colonial Theatre in Phoenixville.

Why do I mention this film? Simple. Global Warming. If you listen and watch the final scene in the film, the Air Force drops the blob in the Artic, because it can't grow in the cold. What if the ice melts and it returns? Think about it. Steve McQueen is gone. Will characters from the Marvel Universe save the planet?

My Favorite Stop in Hammonton, NJ

Hammonton, N J claims to be the blueberry capital of the world. And yes, I do purchase my berries there at Blueberry Bill's Farm. But that's only when our supply runs low. However, since I do most of the grocery shopping for our family, I'm always in search of good food at fair prices. That's why when I take the 30-mile trek to Hammonton to meet up with friends at the Silver Coin Diner, I always make it a point to stop at Bagliani's Italian Food Market. It's located on the main drag in Hammonton. It's one place you can't leave without spending at least $100.

Let me give you a short tour. Upon entering the building, you're greeted on the right by a host of fresh vegetables and produce including large heads of lettuce and crisp celery. Several feet beyond the veggie section are packages of freshly prepared packaged foods, including chicken cutlets, chicken cutlet parmigiana, eggplant parmigiana, tender roast beef as well as turkey with gravy, sausage & peppers, as well as a host of salads including shrimp, chicken cranberry walnut, tuna, and homemade pasta. Take your pick. Above the prepared foods section are well-stocked rows of delicious soups, such as chicken orzo, tomato, butternut squash, and pasta fagioli, to name a few. On top of the soups, you find a host of Italian deserts including cannolis and tiramisu.

We always purchase at least two packages of freshly breaded and cooked chicken cutlets. There are usually four or five pieces in a container, which often covers us for two meals: dinner and lunch the next day. Also, they freeze really well if you're not eating them that day.

Moving past the prepared foods section towards the back of the store is a pair of freezers with an assortment of burgers and seafood products, depending upon the season.

Next to the freezers are the fresh meats cut and packaged by their in-house butchers. You'll find all kinds of top-quality meat including ground beef, steaks, pork, veal, roasts, and brisket, as well as their angus beef hot dogs, which I can't find anywhere else. These are quarter-pound babies and great on the grill. One by itself makes a meal.

To the left of the meat section, you'll find the deli counter, where it really gets crowded at lunchtime. In the large, well-lit case at the deli counter you can view all the various types of sausage made in-store, as well as a wide selection of deli meats and cheeses. This is also the location for ordering and/or picking up preordered sandwiches.

Just past the deli counter you'll find rows and rows of cheese, almost any type you can imagine or ever tasted.

The selection rivals those of markets on 9th street in Philly and has to be the best in South Jersey.

Bagliani's also has an assortment of frozen Italian specialties like tortellini, raviolis, and pizza shells as well as fresh Ricotta. You'll also find some of the best fresh breads and rolls in the area at great prices from places like Del Brunos' bakery and the Formica Bread Company. I usually pick up a half dozen torpedo rolls. Not only are they less expensive than those in the supermarket, but they're also tasty and freeze well. You know great bread makes a great sandwich.

After filling your cart full of these many goodies, you'll find freshly made Federal pretzels at the check-out counter. Why not just top off your groceries with a pair. I often do.

While this may seem like a commercial for Bagliani's, it's not. I just like to stop there.

Overcoming Zakroff's Law

Many folks are familiar with Murphy's Law, "Whatever can go wrong will go wrong." However, as I mentioned in my first book, I have my own law based on years of experience in the audiovisual business. Simply stated, "Zakroff's Law" is "Murphy was an optimist." Let me explain.

In 1976 I was doing work for North American Publishing Company in Philly, creating promotional sound filmstrips for their different business magazines. The President of the firm, Irving Borowsky, was heavily involved with The Jewish Federation in the city. Liking my work, he tapped me to produce a multi-screen, multi-media presentation for the Federation, tied into America's bicentennial celebration.

The presentation would be a six-slide projector, multi-screen show incorporating a 16mm motion picture. It was to be delivered to several hundred attendees at a Federation meeting on a Sunday afternoon at the Sheraton Hotel in downtown Philadelphia.

Knowing it was a big job, I put together a team which included Nate Rosenblatt, a friend and writer who worked for North American, Dan DeSantis, a technical guru, Larry Brown, a professional narrator, and another company, AudioVisual Communications (AVC), to handle the soundtrack. AVC also provided the equipment we needed to program the presentation.

Working with Nate, we developed a 15-minute script for the presentation. Once the script was approved, we matched visuals to illustrate the script. Then, Larry Brown recorded the voice over and AVC scored the soundtrack.

Once this was completed, we assembled the slides into six trays and began programming the show with a complex multimedia device on the third floor of my home office. Since my office wasn't really built for using so much electricity, we had extension cords running all over the house to keep the circuits from popping.

With a great deal of patience, we managed to program the show over the course of several hours. We ran it through it several times to make certain everything was in synch.

Nobody wants to hear you say you're sorry if things went wrong.

Not wanting to be surprised the day of the show, we went to the Sheraton on the Saturday before to make certain everything worked, especially the programming device that ran the entire show. In the control room we hooked up the device and ran the show. We thought we were "home free" except for the actual showing on Sunday.

The next morning my team arrived at Sheraton early. We set up the screens and projectors in the designated ballroom and prepared for a final run-through in advance of the showing. Once the equipment was set up, I turned on the programmer and queued up the show. However, with all the lights and microphones live, we were getting terrible feedback through the ballroom's sound system. The problem never revealed itself on Saturday. The multimedia mechanical marvel was fighting with the sound system. It was loud and distracting. It would never fly.

The only solution was to run the sound separately and not use the hotel's system. With less than two hours to showtime, I drove home, about 45 minutes away, pulled my own Magnavox home system with two speakers out of the stereo cabinet and raced back to the Sheraton. With less than 15 minutes to spare, we hooked up my home sound system on the balcony, set with the speakers to the highest volume and hoped for the best.

As luck would have it, we pulled off the program without a glitch and no one was the wiser for the sound problem.

Aware that "Zakroff's Law" could come into play at any time or place, I always try to have at least a Plan B or Plan C, just in case.

Secrets to writing a successful memoir.

After reading my memoir books, several friends became interested in writing their own and asked for advice along those lines. I was happy to reply. Here's how to do it according to Pete.

First of all, don't wait until you retire to consider writing your memoirs. You may not think you've led an interesting or adventurous life. However, leave that up to your readers to make that final decision. My ultimate purpose was to let my grandchildren know who I was and what I had spent my life doing, besides bringing their parents into this world.

When something happens, take a few notes about it. Write it down on paper in a notebook or open a file on your computer. The event could be the birth of your first child or grandchild, changing jobs, moving to a new town, or the death of a cherished relative.

When an idea pops into my head I come up with a working title and a few bullet points that could be of interest. I put this in a word file on my computer and come back to it when I feel like writing more about the event.

Don't try and write your memoir all at once sitting. It doesn't work. Even novel writers can't do it all at one time. For some it takes years.

The secret of good writing is rewriting. That's something I was taught over 50 years ago.

When I do decide to tackle a story, I put the main facts down first. Then I embellish it a little bit. I may also add some humor, or the lesson learned from the experience. Hopefully I learned something, and the reader will too.

If you're thinking about publishing your work, there are several ways to go.

If you want just a few copies for your immediate family, there are businesses online that will put your work together, add pictures you supply, and make a finished book with a pretty cover on it. These copies can run around $100.00 each or more. It depends on how large your finished work is, the number of pictures you want included, as well as the total number of copies.

If you think your life's story would be of interest to hundreds of people, look up possible agents and publishers in a book called The Writer's Market. A new edition is published every year. You can often find a recent copy at your library.

Don't be surprised if you get rejection letters. That's the nature of the business. Unless you have a unique story to tell or are famous you might not find much interest in taking that approach.

There are also a number of companies who will help you edit, add illustrations, and finish the book for you for a price. They don't provide this service for free, and you might have to purchase several hundred copies of your book as part of the deal.

The best and most cost-effective approach for me was Amazon's Kindle Publishing. After receiving numerous rejection letters, and not wanting to initially print several hundred copies of my first book, my well-published daughter, Laura, suggested I use Kindle Publishing. All I needed to do was format my work into a certain standard size, create artwork (if I wanted any) a front and back cover, and drop the manuscript into their website. It was easy and cost-effective. Check it out if that's the way you want to go. Author's copies are inexpensive, and you can print as many as you want at a time, up to 999 at a time. So, what are you waiting for?

Some Final Thoughts

When I started work on my first book in 2020, I never thought I would be able to write two books, let alone complete a trilogy containing more than 300 tales. If you've read either of my earlier tomes, you know this book was different. Sure, there are additional experiences I never wrote about, as well as numerous observations from a life well-lived. But in this volume, there are also tales told to me by friends that I thought were worth retelling, some of my favorite jokes, as well as examples of my off-the-wall imagination at work.

Since I spent a good part of my life earning a living by writing for other folks, and a paycheck, this endeavor has been for my own personal fun and enjoyment. I love to take a basic story and add some humor or a life-lesson to it. If you learned something from them, great. I also hope you laughed or smiled when reading them as much as I did while writing them.

I've often been asked about how many books I've sold. There have been many. However, selling copies was never the main purpose. It was to tell my story to my grandchildren and their grandchildren to let them know who I was and what I did during my journey through this lifetime. If I accomplished that, this trilogy has been a successful venture.